- Fiqh
- Aḥādīth
- Sīrah
- Tārīkh
- `Aqā'id
- Akhlāq
- Ādāb

An Nasihah Publications

9th edition June 2025

British Library Cataloguing in Publication Data. A catalogue record for this book is available from the British Library.

Every effort has been made to ensure the correctness of the content. The publishers will gladly receive information enabling them to rectify any error or omission in subsequent editions.

An Nasihah Publications Ltd.
58 Buckland Road
Leicester LE5 0NT
United Kingdom

+44 (0)116 2966 442
+44 (0)7414 044 561
www.an-nasihah.com
admin@an-nasihah.com

Distributor in the UK
Azhar Academy, London
020 8911 9797
www.azharacademy.com
sales@azharacademy.com

Distributor in Canada
Hayaat Collection
647-781-7313
hayaat.ca
info@hayaat.ca

Distributors in Australia
Melbourne, Victoria
Mufti Zeeyad Ravat
0499 559 199
zravat@hotmail.com

Distributor in USA
Maktabah Ar-Rahmah
917-565-0709
arrahmahbooks.com
info@arrahmahbooks.com

Printed by Imak Offset in Turkey

Name: ______________________________

Class: ______________________________

Foreword

Over the years, the makātib (religious evening classes) have unanimously played a vital role in preserving the dīn of Allāh (سبحانه وتعالى) by disseminating it to our future generations throughout the world. In England too, in the 1960s when the first immigrants from the Indian subcontinent settled down for a better future and livelihood, a prime objective was to cater for the religious and educational needs of themselves and their offspring. As a result, the first masājid together with makātib were founded.

Initially, the syllabus adopted in these makātib was more or less based on material and syllabus of the Indian subcontinent, as the children were familiar with the Urdu language. Alḥamdulillāh, this went a long way in fulfilling the objectives of the makātib at that time. However, as time passed, the needs of the subsequent generations, together with the ever-changing world, demanded that changes be brought into the syllabus, teaching methods be reviewed and the setup of classes revised, in order to provide the best teaching and learning for our children. The early 1990s witnessed the makātib gradually evolve to a more structured educational entity. A period system for each subject, i.e. fiqh, sīrah, tārīkh, akhlāq and ādāb, was being introduced and the teaching was now being conducted in the English language, which had gradually become the main spoken language of our children.

This transition can be attributed to two main factors. Firstly, many individuals born and bred in England took the path of Islamic education and after graduation began serving their communities as imāms and teachers. Secondly, the availability of Islamic books and literature in the English language became more common and easily accessible. The latter served as a stepping-stone for this transition period.

Foreword

Alḥamdulillāh, the exemplary efforts of the 'ulamā' of South Africa, especially the textbooks prepared by Madrasah Islamia Benoni, Waterval Islamic Institute, and eventually the Tasheel Series and its syllabus prepared by the Jamī'atul 'Ulamā have played a significant role in this regard. Many makātib throughout the UK have benefited from these efforts.

As this new system of teaching became more widespread and well established, many new books and different methods of teaching came to the fore. This was primarily based on teaching experiences and meeting the needs of pupils.

Alḥamdulillāh, the 'Islamic Curriculum' by An Nasihah Publications is also part of this great effort that has come into the public domain. Madrasah An Nasihah has prepared this commendable syllabus with much effort and hard work. It is very pleasing to learn that the young 'ulamā' have worked together cohesively and with perseverance to make this syllabus a reality. They have tried to cover in much detail the core and most important aspects of a child's learning from the age of 4 to 14 years. This has been done adopting a method which makes learning more interesting and enjoyable for children.

I pray that Allāh سبحانه وتعالى accept this work, make it a success and a means of salvation in both worlds. May He enable them to continue authoring beneficial books and literature long into the future. Amīn.

(Shaykh) Muḥammad Saleem Dhorat, Leicester, UK
Islāmic Da'wah Academy

Rajab 1436/May 2015

Foreword

الحمد للہ و الصّلوٰۃ و السلام علی رسول اللہ صلی اللہ تعالی علیہ وسلم ، اما بعد

مجھے بڑی خوشی ہوئی کہ ہمارے ادارے کے عزیز فارغین نے ملکر برطانیہ کے مکاتب میں پڑھنے والے ہمارے مسلمان بچوں کے لئے موجودہ ماحول اور تقاضوں کو سامنے رکھتے ہوئے اور ان نونہالوں کی عمر اور اذہان کا خیال کرتے ہوئے بہترین نصاب مرتب کیا ہے اور احقر کو بھی اس پر نظر ثانی کی درخواست کی گئی ، چونکہ احقر کو پچھلے بیس سال سے یہاں کے مکاتب اور بچوں اور انکی تعلیمی نظام اور نصاب سے واسطہ رہاہے، اور دل میں کئی بار یہ خیال بھی آتا رہا کہ ان مکاتب میں پڑھنے والے ہمارے نونہال بچے بچیاں ان مکاتب میں رہتے ہوئے بہت کچھ اسلامی دینی اھم اھم ضروری تعلیمات اور مسائل کو سیکھ کر جائیں اور عملی نمونہ بنیں اور اسکے لئے ماحول کے تقاضی کے مطابق بہترین نصاب تیار ہو جائے،

الحمد للہ ہمارے ان عزیز دوستوں نے اسلامی درسی نظام کے نام سے یہ آٹھ سالہ نصاب تیار کیا ہے جسے دیکھکر بڑی خوشی ہوئی اور دل سے دعائیں دی کہ اللہ تعالی اسے قبول کرے اور پورے ملک میں پھیلادے اور ہمارے ایک ایک مسلمان بچہ بچی میں ایمانی اسلامی روح پھونک دے، وما ذالک علی اللہ بعزیز

میں نے ان کتابوں کو دیکھا اور اسے برطانوی اذہان کے بچوں کے لئے مفید پایا اور کچھ ضروری مشورے بھی دئے، اس نصاب میں ایک خیال یہ رکھاگیاہیکہ اھم اھم مضامین ایک ہی جلد میں آجائے اور عمر کے اعتبار سے ان مضامین میں زیادتی کی جائے، اور ہر کتاب کے ساتھ ایک تمرین کی بوک بھی رکھی گئی ہے تاکہ اسباق کا مشق بھی ہوتارہے، میری مکاتب کے ذمہ داروں سے درخواست ہے کہ اسے اپنی درسیات میں داخل کریں اور فائدہ اٹھائیں ، اور اسکا ھدیہ بھی دوسری کتابوں کے مقابلہ میں کم رکھاگیا ہے تاکہ ماں باپ پر بوجھ نہ ہو؛ ہماری دعا ہے

تقبل اللہ تعالی سعیھم وجعل سعیھم مشکورا، وینفع بھا الناس جمیعا، آمین

(شیخ الحدیث مولانا) محمد ادریس الفلاحی
ذوالحجہ - اکتوبر

Foreword

All praise belongs to Allāh (سبحانه وتعالى). May His choicest blessings and salutations be upon the beloved Messenger of Allāh (صلى الله عليه وسلم).

It brought me great happiness when I learned that graduates of our institute had embarked on the task of preparing a comprehensive syllabus for the makātib here in the UK, tailoring it for the needs of today's growing generation.
This humble servant has been working within the makātib system for the past twenty years and throughout this many a time a wish came to heart that a complete syllabus be prepared for these young innocent children who can learn the beautiful teachings of Islām in a fun and interactive way.

Alḥamdulillāh when the team at An Nasihah Publications requested that this humble servant take a look at the books that were prepared under the name of The Islamic Curriculum -which spans across eight years- I was delighted when I went through them and prayers escaped my heart that Allāh (سبحانه وتعالى) grant it acceptance and spread it across the lands.

Going through the books, I found them to be of benefit to our children. After giving some points of advice I noted that all the important topics have been combined in one book per year which have corresponding workbooks. The topics are then developed progressively according to the age of the child. It is my humble advice to the responsible people of the makātib to enter these books into their curriculum and take advantage of these books. The price has been kept low so as not to burden parents with large sums of money being spent on books.

Finally I pray to Allāh (سبحانه وتعالى) to accept and reward their efforts granting benefit to all of mankind. Āmīn

(Shaykhul Ḥadīth Mawlānā) Muḥammad Idrīs Falāḥī, Leicester
Senior Lecturer of Ḥadīth at Darul Uloom Leicester

Dhul Ḥijjah 1436/October 2015

Foreword

For many years Raḥma has been operating madāris across the Balkans. After the fall of communism, dīn was still very new to the people hence we initially only had a basic syllabus in place. Over a decade had passed when in 2012 we decided it was time to introduce a more advanced, more informative and interactive syllabus for the students. We contacted An Nasihah Publications expressing our concerns and they gladly took up this noble project.

After a year of consultation and careful planning the 'Islamic Curriculum' series of coursebooks and workbooks were first published. A set of books for the 5 years of maktab were compiled by the team at An Nasihah and then translated into the Albanian language. It covered all the major topics that a Muslim child ought to learn in his/her years at madrasah in a fun and innovative way.

In 2013 the An Nasihah Publications Team launched these books in Albania and Kosovo. Alḥamdulillāh these books have proven to be inspirational. Students and teachers alike have benefited greatly and the Raḥma team of 'Ulamā' have seen a great improvement in the level of education. In 2015 An Nasihah launched a revised edition with additional books for adults too. Just as these books have been successful in Albania and Kosovo, I pray to The Almighty Allāh سبحانه وتعالى that the English version of these books prove to be a greater success in the English speaking world. Āmīn.

(Shaykh) Khalīl Patel, Leicester
Amīr at Raḥma (Mercy)

Rabī' ath-Thānī 1437/January 2016

Foreword

All praise belongs to Allāh (سبحانه وتعالى) and Salutations be upon his honourable Messenger (صلى الله عليه وسلم).

I was greatly pleased upon seeing the Islamic Curriculum by An Nasihah Publications.

Mā shā Allāh this syllabus has been prepared in a child-friendly manner with great effort over the course of eight years.

In addition to this many scholars have looked through it thoroughly.

I pray Allāh (سبحانه وتعالى) accepts this and grants the writers and those associated with it a great recompense. Āmīn

(Shaykh) Abdul Raheem Limbada, Bury

Rabī' ath-Thānī 1437/January 2016

In the name of Allāh (سبحانه وتعالى), All praise belongs to Him and salutations be upon his honourable Messenger (صلى الله عليه وسلم).

The people of knowledge know very well the importance a curriculum has in the Islamic upbringing of the child. Keeping this point in mind Mā shā Allāh a few scholars from Darul Uloom Leicester have put together this simple syllabus which is relevant to the needs and age of our children.

This humble one had a brief look over the books and was greatly pleased.

May Allāh (سبحانه وتعالى) grant this syllabus acceptance and benefit the ummah through it.

Muftī Mūsā Badat, Dewsbury

Rabī' ath-Thānī 1437/January 2016

Foreword

الحمد للہ برطانیہ میں مکاتب کا نظام ایک معیاری اور مثالی صورت اختیار کر گیا ہے، اور اکثر شہروں اور قصبات میں بہترین مکاتب وجود میں آگئے ہیں، اس لئے ضرورت تھی کہ یہاں کے مکاتب کے لئے کوئی معیاری نصاب ترتیب دیا جائے۔ مبارکبادی اور شکریہ کی مستحق ہیں لیسٹر کے علماء کی وہ جماعت جنہوں نے برسوں کی محنت اور توجہ سے آٹھ سالہ ایک نصاب ترتیب دے کر امت مسلمہ اور خصوصا اہل برطانیہ پر عظیم احسان کیا۔ چونکہ یہ نصاب انگریزی زبان میں ہے، اس لئے میں اس سے استفادہ نہ کرسکا، لیکن اکابر علماء نے اس پر نظر فرمائی اور اس کو بہتر سے بہتر بنانے کے لئے اپنی اپنی رائے مرحمت فرمائی۔ امید ہے کہ یہ نصاب ملک کے مکاتب کے لئے ایک بہترین نصاب ہوگا، اورانشاء اللہ مرتبین کے لئے صدقۂ جاریہ اور ذخیرۂ نجات ہوگا۔

بعض اہل علم نے اس کے مطالعہ کے بعد فرمایا کہ: بہت جامع نصاب ہے ،ایک ہی کتاب میں مختلف سات قسم کے مضامین جمع کئے گئے ہیں، اس میں طلباء اور اساتذہ کے لئے آسانی اور بڑی سہولت ہے۔

اللہ تعالی سے دلی دعا ہے کہ ان نوجوان علماء کی محنت کو شرف قبولیت عطا فرمائے، اور مکاتب کے ذمہ داروں اور صدر مدرسین کو ان کی حوصلہ افزائی کی توفیق مرحمت فرمائے۔
اللہ کرے پورے ملک کا ایک نصاب ہو ،اوریہاں کے ارباب انتظام کو یہ مناسب لگے تو اور اسی کو داخل نصاب کرلیں۔ اور اس معاملہ میں کسی تعصب کے بغیر غور کریں کہ اس نصاب کو اپنے مکاتب میں داخل کیا جائے یا نہیں؟ اس لئے کہ عصبیت بڑے سے بڑے ہنر اورمفید سے مفید کام کو بھی قبول کرنے سے مانع بنتی ہے ۔

اس نصاب کی تیاری میں جن جن علماء نے محنت فرمائی اللہ تعالی ان کو دارین میں بہترین بدلہ عطافرمائے، آمین ۔

(مولانا) مرغوب احمد لاجپوری ۔ ڈیوزبری
جمادی الثانیة - مارچ

Foreword

In the name of Allāh (سبحانه وتعالى) the Most Beneficent, the Most Merciful.

Iqra' was the first word of revelation from the Lord of the Worlds to our Beloved Messenger Muḥammad (صلى الله عليه وسلم) through the Angel Jibra'īl. This was the first lesson to light the lantern of knowledge to mankind which were drowned in ignorance and darkness and it is through this very word that we see many libraries in existence today brimming with books.

Blessed are those scholars and thinkers who, in every era, worked tirelessly for the growing needs of the future generation to protect their knowledge and actions.

From these very scholars our young graduates of Britain from An Nasihah Publications came together to prepare this year by year syllabus according to the needs of our children.

I strongly feel that the children's minds and hearts will find them appealing and this syllabus, along with filling a gap, will be a means of fulfilling the need.

May Allāh (سبحانه وتعالى) increase the team in knowledge and practice and make these books beneficial and full of blessings. Āmīn

Shaykhul Ḥadīth Mawlānā Muḥammad Ayyūb Sūrtī
Senior lecturer of ḥadīth at Darul Uloom Falāḥ e Darayn, India
Director of Majlis e Dawatul Haq, UK

Jumadā ath-Thāniyah 1437/March 2016

Foreword

Alḥamdulillāh, I was very pleased to meet the group of scholars from An Nasihah Publications. The Islamic Curriculum books have been compiled in a very beautiful and easy-to-understand method.

May Allāh سبحانه وتعالى accept the hard work of the young 'ulamā' and make it beneficial for our youngsters and students of maktabs and madrasahs.

I would really recommend these books to all our children who want to know about our beautiful religion.

Shaykh Muftī Saiful Islām
Founder, Principal and Director of Jāmiah Khātamun Nabiyeen (JKN), Bradford, UK
Editor of the family magazine 'Al Mu'min'

Jumadā ath-Thāniyah 1437/March 2016

The presentation of these books is dyslexia-friendly and they will appeal to all the children who use them. The layout is clear and uncluttered, with key texts often contained within information boxes. The use of pastel colours and clear text is helpful to children who find reading difficult.

Fiona Hossack
Teaching Coordinator
Leicester Dyslexia Association

Foreword

Alḥamdulillāh this curriculum by An Nasihah Publications is a unique gift for the growing need of today's generation.

The team from Darul Uloom Leicester have worked tirelessly to make these books fun and engaging according to the age and need of the child.

I humbly request the management of the institutes to implement this curriculum into their madāris & Islamic schools through which our children will benefit greatly in shā Allāh.

Together the syllabus can go from strength to strength through your constructive feedback making it a Ṣadaqah Jāriyah for us all.

May Allah accept this humble effort. Āmīn

Mawlana Ismail Ahmad Patel
Principal and founder of Darul Uloom Leicester

Sha'bān 1437/May 2016

Testimonials

Testimonials obtained from parents whose children are studying the Islamic Curriculum.

"Having taken time out to look over the books, I find them to be inspiring, student-friendly and highly educational. It is clearly well-researched and covers all the needed topics. May Allāh سبحانه وتعالى reward all those included in the publication of these books."

"Mā shā Allāh the books cover a wide range of topics and contain essential material on every subject. This should give a solid foundation in obtaining necessary knowledge of dīn."

"Very pleased with the coursebooks. They're very child and parent-friendly for the whole family to learn and brush up on basic knowledge, Mā shā Allāh. Encourages one to learn."

"I'd like to thank you and your team for all the time and effort you have put into making these Islamic books for our children. The books are very educational, beautiful to look at and easy to understand. I myself will gain knowledge from the books as well as the children."

"This comprehensive syllabus program for the madāris on preparing children for life and beyond is published beautifully with colour & illustration. The way the syllabus has been printed in the first few pages gives parents an insight into what ages will learn what subjects. I see my children excited to learn the different subjects, due to it being filled with fun and activities. It is also beneficial to us, parents, who haven't been lucky enough to learn in this manner, especially with regard to the aḥādīth. May the Almighty reward everyone who made this publication possible, āmīn."

Preface

All praise is due to Allāh (سبحانه وتعالى), Lord of the heavens and earth. May peace and blessings be upon our Noble Messenger, Muḥammad (صلى الله عليه وسلم).

It is a great blessing of Allāh (سبحانه وتعالى) that He has made this dream into a reality. For many years our team at An Nasīhah have been working on a comprehensive syllabus program for the madāris to prepare the pupils for life and beyond. We wanted to give our children a series of books with colourful yet fruitful content to allow them to grasp the key elements of their dīn with love and devotion.

Alḥamdulillāh when Moulāna Khalīl (May Allāh (سبحانه وتعالى) protect him) approached us in 2012 on behalf of Raḥma (Mercy) with a proposal of setting out something similar for the pupils of Albania, we were able to see the benefits of such a system. Alḥamdulillāh 50 thousand books were printed and rolled out across all the madāris operating under Raḥma (Mercy) in Albania and Kosovo. The feedback we received from the teachers and pupils was highly positive. This motivated us to push for the initial English version and - with all praise to Allāh (سبحانه وتعالى) - after many hard years of effort from our team, you now have the books before you.

Each of the eight books in the series corresponds with a workbook to assist in understanding the topics thoroughly. Seven subjects are covered progressively across the years.

Preface

At the end of the eight-year course, In shā Allāh pupils will have mastered the five pillars of Islām along with a large amount of fiqh necessary for them to lead their lives as Muslims. They will have memorised 85 aḥādīth in Arabic and English, understood the basic creed ('aqā'id) of a Muslim, covered approximately 100 akhlāq & ādāb, learnt about many Prophets, covered the whole life of our Beloved Messenger Muḥammad (صلى الله عليه وسلم) along with the 4 Khulafā and many more anecdotes and achievements from the annals of our history.

I pray Allāh (سبحانه وتعالى) accepts this humble work in His court, rewards all those who were part of this publication in any way, their families and their associates with His pleasure and success in both worlds. Āmīn

If you find any fault, then correct it I pray,
For no one is faultless except Allāh
(Imām Jalāl-ud-dīn Suyūṭī)

Shaykh Muḥammad Yaḥyā
Director - An Nasihah Publications

Rabi' al-Awwal 1436/January 2015

Transliteration Key

Vowels

A	Short vowel as in 'Ago'	I	Short vowel as in 'Sit'
Ā	Long Vowel as in 'Heart'	Ī	Long vowel as in 'See'
AY	Diphthong as in 'Page'	AW	Diphthong as in 'Home'
'	Abrupt start or pause	U	Short vowel as in 'Put'
Ū	Long vowel as in 'Food'		

Consonants

ب	B	'B', no 'H' attached	ص	Ṣ	'S' with full mouth
ت	T	Soft 'T', no 'H' attached	ض	Ḍ	'D' with full mouth, using sides of tongue
ث	TH	'TH' as in 'Thin'	ط	Ṭ	'T' with full mouth
ح	Ḥ	'H' Guttural Sound	ظ	Ẓ	'DH' as in 'Dhuhr' with full mouth
خ	KH	'KH' Very guttural, no usage of tongue	ع	'	Guttural sound - Accompanies vowel
د	D	Soft 'D', no 'H' attached	غ	GH	'GH' Very guttural, no usage of tongue
ذ	DH	'DH' as in 'Adhān'	ق	Q	'K' with back of tongue raised
س	S	'S' only, not 'Z'	و	W	'W' read, not silent
ش	SH	'SH' as in 'Shin'	ى	Y	'Y' only, not 'I'

Note: Double consonants must be pronounced with emphasis on both letters without pause. e.g. Allāhumma should be read al-lāhum-ma.

(سبحانه وتعالى)
Subḥānahū wa ta'ālā
May He be glorified

(صلى الله عليه وسلم)
Ṣallallāhu 'alayhi wasallam
Allāh's peace and mercy be upon him

(عليه السلام)
'Alayhis salām
Peace be upon him

(رضي الله عنه)
Raḍiyallāhu 'anhu
May Allāh be pleased with him

Contents

Syllabus

CURRENT BOOK

Coursebook	C 1	C 2	C 3	C 4
Guide Age Range:	6 - 7yrs	7 -8yrs	8 - 9yrs	9 - 10yrs
Fiqh	Basic Introduction to Five Pillars of Islām Shahādah, Ṣalāh, Zakāh, Ṣawm & Ḥajj Introduction to Ṭahārah Method of Wuḍū'	Methods of Staying Clean: Istinjā', Wuḍū' and Ghusl. Wuḍū' in Detail: Farā'iḍ, Sunan, Mustaḥabbāt, Makrūhāt and Nawāqiḍ. Brief Introduction to Tayammum Method of Ṣalāh for Boys and Girls	Keywords Types of Najāsah Ghusl: Farā'iḍ, Sunan and Method Rak'āt of Ṣalāh Conditions of Ṣalāh Nawāqiḍ of Ṣalāh Method of Ṣalāh Ṣalātul Witr Ṣalātul Qaṣr Ṣalātul Musāfir Ṣalātul Mariḍ	Masaḥ 'Alal Khuffayn Masaḥ on Wounds Wajibāt of Ṣalāh Sajdah as-Sahw Ṣawm Tarāwīḥ
Aḥādīth	5 Aḥādīth	5 Aḥādīth	10 Aḥādīth	10 Aḥādīth
	Feeding the Hungry Helping Others Doing Things Slowly Cleanliness Truth	Truth Salām Using the Right Hand Drinking Whilst Sitting Kindness to Neighbours	Ṣalāh Love for Others Steadfastness Life This World Du'ā' Guests Mercy Modesty Shukr	Feeding Others, No to Racism, Good Character Thanking Others, Friends, Kindness Trust, Keys to Paradise, Dhikr Du'ā'

C 5	C 6 Boys	C 6 Girls	C 7	C 8
10 - 11yrs	11 - 12yrs	11 - 12yrs	12 - 13yrs	13 - 14yrs
Miscellaneous Points of Wuḍū', Tayammum in Detail Sunan of Ṣalāh Forbidden and Disliked Times of Ṣalāh Ṣalāh of a Masbūq Qaḍā Ṣalāh 'īd Ṣalāh Ḥajj and 'Umrah Ziyārah	Types of Water Impurities and Cleaning Methods Maturity in Boys Wājib Acts of Ṣalāh Masā'il of Being an Imām Janā'iz: Method of Ghusl for the Deceased, Shrouding and Burial Jumu'ah Ṣalāh Adhān and Iqāmah	Types of Water Impurities and Cleaning Methods Maturity in Girls Masā'il of Ḥayḍ, Nifās and Istiḥāḍah Wājib Acts of Ṣalāh Janā'iz: Method of Ghusl for the Deceased, Shrouding and Burial	Mustaḥabbāt and Makrūhāt of Ṣalāh Sutrah Sajdah Tilāwah Taḥarrī, Qaṣr Ṣalāh, Ṣalātul Mariḍ and Ma'dhūr, Ṣalātul Kusūf/Khusūf Zakāh, Inheritance I'tikāf, Laylatul Qadr Ḥalāl Foods, Cross Contamination, List of Ḥalāl and Ḥarām Animals, Seafood, Uḍḥiyah	Nafl Ṣalāh, Khushū', Ṣalāh with Jamā'ah Nikāḥ: Choosing a Spouse, Relations Before Marriage List of Maḥārim, Mahr, Walīmah Ṭalāq: Different Types of Ṭalāq, 'Iddah Buyū': Ijārah, Ribā and Gambling Taqlīd: Different Schools of Fiqh, References from Ḥadīth
10 Aḥādīth	15 Aḥādīth	15 Aḥādīth	15 Aḥādīth	15 Aḥādīth
Promises, Tongue Ghībah, Intoxicants Beauty of a Person's Islām, Carrying Tales 99 Names of Allāh (سبحانه وتعالى) Importance of the Last 3 Sūrahs (Mu'awwidhāt) Speaking Good, Good Character	Major Sins, Pride, Good Character, Health and Free Time Truth and Lies, Love for the Messenger (صلى الله عليه وسلم) Islām is Based upon 5 Pillars, Qur'ān as an Intercessor Ṣalāh at its Correct Time, Kindness to Parents, Gatherings, Good Actions, Ṣadaqah, Ramaḍān, Friendship	Major Sins, Pride, Good Character, Health and Free Time Truth and Lies, Love for the Messenger (صلى الله عليه وسلم) Islām is Based upon 5 Pillars, Qur'ān as an Intercessor Ṣalāh at its Correct Time, Kindness to Parents, Gatherings, Good Actions, Ṣadaqah, Ramaḍān, Friendship	People of Jannah and Jahannam, Ghībah Siwāk, Not Faulting Food, Modesty, Forgiveness of Sins, Lies Appreciate Blessings, Laylatul Qadr, Durūd, Signs of a Mu'min, Stopping Others from Evil, Ṣalāh with Jamā'ah, Du'ā', Dhikr	Not Having Hatred for Anyone. Spending for the Sake of Allāh (سبحانه وتعالى), Disliked Actions, Salām upon Entering Rights of a Muslim, Status of a Mu'min, Reward of Patience, Forgiving Others, True Wealth, Islām is Easy Sweetness of Īmān, Ṣalāh, Closeness to Allāh (سبحانه وتعالى), Power of Allāh (سبحانه وتعالى), Being Self-sufficient

Syllabus

CURRENT BOOK

Coursebook	C 1	C 2	C 3	C 4
Guide Age Range:	6 - 7yrs	7 -8yrs	8 - 9yrs	9 - 10yrs
Sīrah	Childhood of Our Beloved Messenger Muḥammad صلى الله عليه وسلم His صلى الله عليه وسلم Youth. Marriage to Khadījah رضي الله عنها The Children of our Beloved Messenger صلى الله عليه وسلم	In the Cave of Ḥirā The First Revelation The First Believers Open Call to Islām Persecutions Faced by Muslims	Migration to Abyssinia Two Great Warriors Accept Islām A Different way The Boycott The Year of Sadness The Journey to Ṭā'if Inviting the Arab Tribes Al-Isrā' and al-Mi'rāj	The Pledge at 'Aqabah, Hijrah Journey, Arrival in Madīnah Munawwarah Treaties with the Jews, The Hypocrites Battles of Badr, Uḥud & Aḥzāb
Tārīkh	Ādam عليه السلام Nūh عليه السلام	Hūd عليه السلام Ṣāliḥ عليه السلام	Ibrāhīm عليه السلام Ismā'īl عليه السلام Isḥāq عليه السلام	Ya'qūb عليه السلام Yūsuf عليه السلام
'Aqā'id	Articles of Faith Qualities of Allāh سبحانه وتعالى Allāh سبحانه وتعالى the Provider, Allāh سبحانه وتعالى The Merciful	Allāh سبحانه وتعالى the Protector, The All Hearing, The All Seeing, The One Angels Revealed Books The Qur'ān	Messengers Qiyāmah Minor Signs List of the Major Signs	Major signs in Detail: Mahdi, Dajjāl, 'Īsā عليه السلام Ya'jūj Ma'jūj, The Beast The Sun Rising from the West, The Smoke, Landslides Blowing of the Trumpet, The Day of Qiyāmah, Mīzān and The Bridge

C 5	C 6 Boys	C 6 Girls	C 7	C 8
10 - 11yrs	11 - 12yrs	11 - 12yrs	12 - 13yrs	13 - 14yrs
Treaty of Ḥudaybiyyah, Bay'ah ar-Riḍwān, The Message of Islām Spreads, 'Umratul Qaḍā Conquest of Makkah, The Battle of Ḥunain, The March to Tabūk The Farewell Pilgrimage, The Messenger صلى الله عليه وسلم Leaves the World	Shamā'il Abū Bakr رضي الله عنه His Life and Work	Shamā'il Abū Bakr رضي الله عنه His Life and Work The Mothers of the Believers	Shamā'il 'Umar رضي الله عنه His Life and Work	Shamā'il 'Uthmān رضي الله عنه 'Ali رضي الله عنه Their Lives and Works
Mūsā عليه السلام 'Īsā عليه السلام	Dāwūd عليه السلام Sulaymān عليه السلام Yūnus عليه السلام Introduction to Islamic History The Umayyads	Dāwūd عليه السلام Sulaymān عليه السلام Yūnus عليه السلام Introduction to Islamic History The Umayyads	Zakariyyā عليه السلام Yaḥyā عليه السلام The Abbāsids	Ayyūb عليه السلام Andalusia (Muslim Spain) The Crusades The Ottomans
Death, Journey after death, Jannah, Description, Seeing Allāh سبحانه وتعالى, Actions that Lead to Jannah Jahannam: Description, Actions that Lead to Jahannam A'rāf, introduction to Taqdīr, our Beliefs with Regard to Allāh سبحانه وتعالى Our Beliefs with Regard to the Prophets and the Ṣaḥābah	Ahlus Sunnah wal Jamā'ah, Beliefs with Regard to Prophethood The Ṣaḥābah & their Rankings, Four Khulafā Asharah Mubasharah. The Awliyā', Mu'jizāt and Karāmāt Isrā' and Mi'rāj	Ahlus Sunnah wal Jamā'ah, Beliefs with Regard to Prophethood The Ṣaḥābah & their Rankings, Four Khulafā Asharah Mubasharah. The Awliyā', Mu'jizāt and Karāmāt Isrā' and Mi'rāj	Qaḍā' and Qadr Evil Eye The World as a Place of Means Life after Death Barzakh Resurrection	Attributes (Ṣifāt) of Allāh سبحانه وتعالى Istiwā' Īmān Consulting the 'Ulamā'

Syllabus

CURRENT BOOK

Coursebook	C 1	C 2	C 3	C 4
Guide Age Range:	6 - 7yrs	7 -8yrs	8 - 9yrs	9 - 10yrs
Akhlāq	Respect Cleanliness Politeness in Speech Smiling Starting from the Right Hand Side	Keeping Promises Being Thankful Spreading Salām Helping in Good Things Kindness to Animals	Thinking Good of Others Sharing Kindness to Parents Speaking the Truth Saying a Good Word	Trust Seeking Permission Before Entering Removing Harm from the Road Being a Good Neighbour
Ādāb	Ādāb of: Eating Drinking Sleeping, Waking up Using the Washroom	Ādāb of: Greeting Entering a House Speaking Sneezing Yawning	Ādāb of: Travelling Studying Qur'ān Walking Masjid	Ādāb of: Du'ā' Dressing Guests & Hosts Sitting in a Gathering Istinjā

C 5	C 6 Boys	C 6 Girls	C 7	C 8
10 - 11yrs	11 - 12yrs	11 - 12yrs	12 - 13yrs	13 - 14yrs
Asking Advice (Mashwarah) Patience Ties of Kinship Exchanging Gifts and Honouring the Guest Virtues of Dhikr	Oppression and Bullying Envy Ghībah Pride Following the Sunnah	Oppression and Bullying Envy Ghībah Pride Following the Sunnah	Spreading Rumours Value of Time Virtues of Knowledge Benefits of Durūd and Ṣalawāt	Shortness of this Life Taqwā Tawakkul Tawbah Modesty in Gaze
Ādāb of: Ghusl Social Interaction Writing Siwāk Visiting the Sick	Ādāb of: Moderation in Expenditure Importance of a Woman in Society Adhān 'Īdayn Jumu'ah Personal Hygiene	Ādāb of: Adhān Modesty in Dress Moderation in Expenditure Importance of a Woman in Society Personal Hygiene	5 Branches of Faith: Mu'āsharat; Social Manners Taking Oaths, Answering Questions, Using a Mobile Phone and the Internet. Walking with Elders Beginning from the Right when Serving Informing Dependants of one's Whereabouts Interaction with non-Muslims, Condolences	Mu'āmalāt: Debate and Discussions Nikāh, Transactions Ādāb for the Seller Ādāb for the Buyer General Ādāb of Shopping

اَلْحَمْدُ لِلّٰهِ رَبِّ الْعَالَمِيْنَ
وَالصَّلَاةُ وَالسَّلَامُ عَلٰى نَبِيِّنَا مُحَمَّدٍ
وَعَلٰى اٰلِهٖ وَصَحْبِهٖ أَجْمَعِيْنَ

بِسْمِ اللّٰهِ الرَّحْمٰنِ الرَّحِيْمِ

Fiqh

Learning Objectives

At the end of this unit pupils will be able to:

Define the key words of fiqh.

Understand types of najāsah (impurity).

Know the difference between the farā'iḍ & sunan of ghusl.

Summarise ṣalāh, the conditions before and during ṣalāh, nawāqiḍ and method.

Show when and how Ṣalātul Witr, Ṣalātul Qaṣr and Ṣalātul Mariḍ are performed.

Key words

TERMINOLOGY TREE

Nawāqiḍ

Makrūh

Ṭahārah

Mubāḥ

Ḥarām

Makrūh Taḥrīmī

Wājib

Farḍ

Mustaḥabb

Sunnah Mu'akkadah

Sunnah Ghayr Mu'akkadah

Ṭahārah:	Purity
Farḍ:	Compulsory/Something you must do.
Wājib:	Necessary - Next to farḍ.
Sunnah Mu'akkadah:	An action which Rasūlullāh صلى الله عليه وسلم did regularly.
Sunnah Ghayr Mu'akkadah:	An action which Rasūlullāh صلى الله عليه وسلم did sometimes.
Mustaḥab:	Preferable/Good to do.
Mubāh:	Allowed/Permitted
Makrūh:	Disliked
Makrūh Taḥrīmī:	Highly disliked and close to ḥarām.
Ḥarām:	Forbidden/Not allowed
Nawāqiḍ:	Acts that break/ nullify something.

Types of Najāsah

Najāsah: Impurity

Two types

Najāsah Ḥaqīqī is that impurity which can be seen.

- **Najāsah Ghalīẓah** The greater impurity such as blood, urine, stool etc.
- **Najāsah Khafīfah** The lighter impurity such as the urine of ḥalāl animals.

Najāsah Ḥukmī is that impurity which cannot be seen.

- **Ḥadath Akbar** When a person is in need of ghusl.
- **Ḥadath Aṣghar** When a person is in need of wuḍū'.

Ghusl

Ghusl is a bath which we must take when we are in the state of impurity.

Three Farā'iḍ of Ghusl

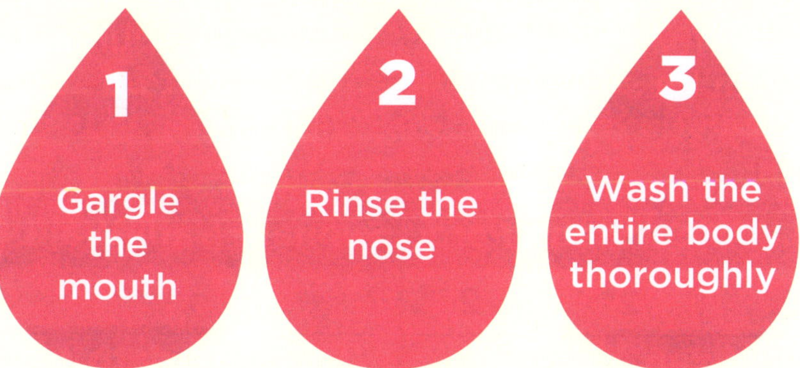

Wash in such a way that not a single hair is left dry.

Five Sunan of Ghusl

1. Make intention to become pure
2. Wash hands
3. Wash the private parts
4. Make wuḍū'
5. Pass water over the body thrice

When washing the body in ghusl, wash the head first, then wash the right side of the body and then wash the left side.

Fiqh

Ṣalāh

Ṣalāh is one of the most important actions in our daily life. Allāh سبحانه وتعالى invites us to talk to Him five times a day. Ṣalāh is the first thing we will be asked about on the Day of Qiyāmah.

The table below contains a breakdown of the total number of rak'āt for each of the five daily ṣalāh.

Ṣalāh	Sunnah	Farḍ	Sunnah	Nafl	Wājib	Nafl
Fajr	2*	2				
Ẓuhr	4*	4	2*	2		
'Aṣr	4	4				
Maghrib		3	2*	2		
'Ishā'	4	4	2*	2	3	2

* Sunnah Mu'akkadah

Jumu'ah ṣalāh will replace ẓuhr on Friday when performed with jamā'ah. More details on jumu'ah can be found in Coursebook 6.

Ṣalāh	Sunnah	Farḍ	Sunnah	Nafl
Jumu'ah	4	2	4*+ 2*	2

Ṣalāh

Conditions before ṣalāh

1. Perform ghusl if necessary.
2. Perform wuḍū' if necessary.
3. Cover the satr (parts which must be covered).

   a. Male satr: from the navel to the knees, including the knees

   b. Female satr: the whole body except the face, hands and feet.
4. Make sure that the body and clothes are clean.

   (They should not have impurities.)
5. Make sure that the place is clean.
6. Face the Qiblah.
7. Pray in the correct time.
8. Make an intention.

Ṣalāh

Conditions in/during ṣalāh
(Farḍ acts in ṣalāh)

1. Takbīr Taḥrīmah - The first takbīr when starting ṣalāh.
2. Qiyām - The standing position in ṣalāh.
3. Qirā'ah - Reciting the Qur'ān.
4. Rukū' - Bowing down.
5. Sujūd - Prostration on the ground.
6. Qa'dah Akhīrah – Last sitting before salām for the duration of tashahhud.

Ṣalāh

Some acts which break Ṣalāh

(Nawāqiḍ of ṣalāh)

1. To eat or drink.
2. To make any type of unnecessary noise.
3. To do 'amal kathīr: A) an action which if people were to see would think that the person is not in ṣalāh, B) to do an action three times in one position.
4. To talk in ṣalāh.
5. To not let the feet touch the ground, even once, throughout the entire sajdah.
6. Opening of a quarter of any limb from the satr for the duration of one rukn.
7. Laughing aloud in ṣalāh.
8. To turn the chest away from the Qiblah.
9. Making an error in the qirā'ah of the Qur'ān which changes the meaning.
10. To step ahead of the imām during ṣalāh.

Ṣalāh

Method of ṣalāh for boys

1) Lift both hands up to the ears with thumbs in line with the earlobes and palms facing the qiblah, say: اَللّٰهُ أَكْبَرُ

2) Place the right hand on top of the left below the navel whilst grasping the wrist with the thumb and small finger, placing the three remaining fingers closely together on the forearm.

3) Read A) Du'ā' al-Istiftāḥ (Thanā'), B) Ta'awwudh, C) Tasmiyah, D) Sūrah Fātiḥah, E) at least one long āyah or three short āyāt of the Qur'ān.

4) Saying اَللّٰهُ أَكْبَرُ Go into rukū'. In rukū' the back and head should be kept in a straight line and the fingers spread, grasping the knees.

5) Recite سُبْحَانَ رَبِّيَ الْعَظِيْمِ at least three times in rukū'.

6) Saying سَمِعَ اللّٰهُ لِمَنْ حَمِدَهٗ rise from rukū' followed by رَبَّنَا وَلَكَ الْحَمْدُ.

7) Saying اَللّٰهُ اَكْبَرْ go into sajdah. Place the knees first, followed by the hands then the nose and forehead. In sajdah the thighs and stomach should not touch. The fingers should be kept close together with the elbows raised from the ground and away from the sides. Recite سُبْحَانَ رَبِّيَ الْاَعْلٰى at least three times in sajdah.

8) Saying اَللّٰهُ اَكْبَرْ sit in the sitting position with composure for a little while. Sit on the left foot with the right foot being upright with its toes facing the Qiblah.

9) Go into the second sajdah saying اَللّٰهُ اَكْبَرْ and recite the same tasbīḥ as the first sajdah.

Ṣalāh

10) Saying ٱللهُ أَكْبَرُ stand up for the second rak'ah by lifting the forehead, followed by the nose then the hands and finally the knees.

11) Perform the second rak'ah exactly as the first one without reciting Du'ā' al-Istiftāḥ or Ta'awwudh.

After the second sajdah of the second rak'ah, sit and recite tashahhud. When reaching أَشْهَدُ أَنْ لَّا إِلٰهَ form a ring with the middle finger and the thumb. Lift the index finger, indicating to the oneness of Allāh سبحانه وتعالى. Drop the index finger when reaching إِلَّا اللهُ. The other fingers will be curled in line with the middle finger.

Ṣalāh

12) In the last rak'ah of every ṣalāh sit and recite tashahhud followed by Ibrāhīmiyyah (Durūd) and du'ā'.

13) End the ṣalāh by saying اَلسَّلَامُ عَلَيْكُمْ وَرَحْمَةُ الله by turning the face towards the right shoulder and repeating it whilst turning towards the left shoulder. The head should turn to the extent that the cheek can be seen by the person behind.

In the third and fourth rak'ah of farḍ ṣalāh, recite Sūrah al-Fātiḥah only without reciting a sūrah after it. However, if you are not praying a farḍ ṣalāh but are praying a sunnah Ṣalāh, then Sūrah al-Fātiḥah will be followed by a sūrah in every rak'ah.

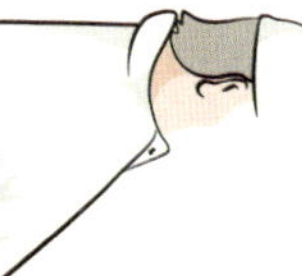

Fiqh

Ṣalāh

Method of ṣalāh for girls

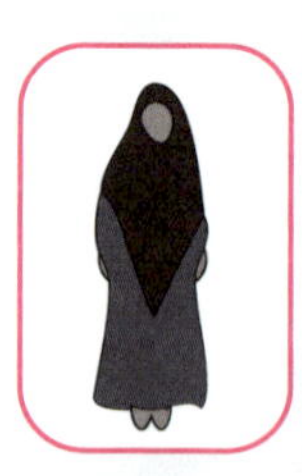

1) Ensure the hair is fully covered.

2) Lift both hands up to the shoulders and say: اَللّٰهُ اَكْبَرُ

3) Place the right hand on top of the left on the chest with both palms facing towards the chest and the fingers being kept close together.

4) Read A) Du'ā' al-Istiftāḥ (Thanā'), B) Ta'awwudh, C) Tasmiyah, D) Sūrah Fātiḥah, E) at least one long āyah or three short āyāt of the Qur'ān.

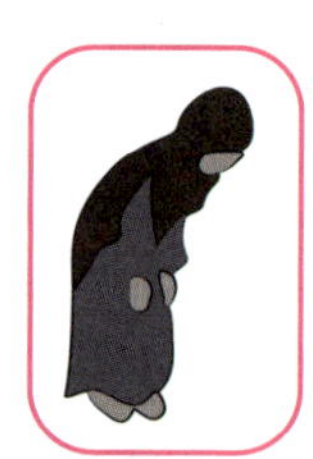

5) Saying اَللّٰهُ اَكْبَرُ go into rukū'. In rukū' the back should be slightly bent in order to be able to touch the knees with the fingers being kept close together. (In rukū', sajdah and qa'dah the fingers will be kept close to each other.) The ankles should also be together. Recite سُبْحَانَ رَبِّيَ الْعَظِيْمِ at least three times.

Ṣalāh

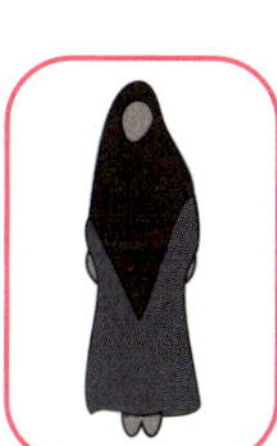

6) Saying سَمِعَ اللّٰهُ لِمَنْ حَمِدَهٗ rise from rukū' followed by رَبَّنَا وَلَكَ الْحَمْدُ

7) Saying اَللّٰهُ اَكْبَرْ go into sajdah. Place the knees first followed by the hands and then the nose and forehead. In sajdah the body should be kept close together, with arms placed on the ground and the thighs and stomach should touch. Both the feet should face the right.

8) Recite سُبْحَانَ رَبِّيَ الْاَعْلٰى three times and saying اَللّٰهُ اَكْبَرْ sit in the sitting position with composure for a little while. Sit on the floor with both feet facing towards the right, with the right thigh on the left thigh.

9) Go into the second sajdah saying اَللّٰهُ اَكْبَرْ and recite the same tasbīḥ as the first sajdah.

Ṣalāh

10) Saying اَللّٰهُ اَكْبَرْ stand up for the second rak‘ah by lifting the forehead, followed by the nose then the hands and finally the knees.

11) Perform the second rak‘ah exactly as the first one without reciting Du'ā' al-Istiftāḥ or Ta'awwudh.

After the second sajdah of the second rak‘ah, sit and recite tashahhud. When reaching أَشْهَدُ أَنْ لَّا إِلٰهَ form a ring with the middle finger and the thumb. Lift the index finger, indicating to the oneness of Allāh سبحانه وتعالى. Drop the index finger when reaching إِلَّا اللّٰهُ. The other fingers will be curled in line with the middle finger.

Ṣalāh

12) In the last rak'ah of every ṣalāh sit with the fingers being kept close together and recite tashahhud followed by Ibrāhīmiyyah (Durūd) and du'ā'. Sit on the floor with both feet facing towards the right, with the right thigh on the left thigh.

13) End the ṣalāh by saying اَلسَّلَامُ عَلَيْكُمْ وَرَحْمَةُ اللهِ by turning the face towards the right shoulder and repeating it whilst turning towards the left shoulder.

In the third and fourth rak'ah of farḍ ṣalāh, recite Sūrah al-Fātiḥah only without reciting a sūrah after it. However, if you are not praying a farḍ ṣalāh but are praying a sunnah Ṣalāh, then Sūrah al-Fātiḥah will be followed by a sūrah in every rak'ah.

Ṣalāh

Ṣalātul Witr

1 Salātul Witr is prayed after the farḍ of 'Ishā'.

2 It cannot be read before the farḍ of 'Ishā'.

3 There are 3 rak'āt in Ṣalātul Witr.

4 It is wājib.

5 Ṣalātul Witr is prayed daily.

6 The first two rak'āt of Witr are exactly the same as other rak'āt of ṣalāh. However, in the third rak'ah of Witr Ṣalāh after Sūrah Fātiḥah, a sūrah will be read. We then lift our hands and do an extra takbīr. Thereafter we will recite Du'ā' Qunūt.

7 In Ramaḍān it will be prayed with jamā'ah behind the imām after the Tarāwīḥ Ṣalāh.

Ṣalāh

Du'ā' Qunūt

اَللّٰهُمَّ إِنَّا نَسْتَعِيْنُكَ، وَنَسْتَغْفِرُكَ، وَنُؤْمِنُ بِكَ وَنَتَوَكَّلُ عَلَيْكَ

وَنُثْنِيْ عَلَيْكَ الْخَيْرَ، وَنَشْكُرُكَ وَلَا نَكْفُرُكَ وَنَخْلَعُ وَنَتْرُكُ مَنْ

يَّفْجُرُكَ، اَللّٰهُمَّ إِيَّاكَ نَعْبُدُ، وَلَكَ نُصَلِّيْ وَنَسْجُدُ، وَإِلَيْكَ نَسْعٰى

وَنَحْفِدُ، نَرْجُوْ رَحْمَتَكَ، وَنَخْشٰى عَذَابَكَ، إِنَّ عَذَابَكَ

بِالْكُفَّارِ مُلْحِقٌ وَصَلَّى اللّٰهُ عَلَى النَّبِيِّ الْكَرِيْمِ

O Allāh! We beg help from You alone, ask forgiveness from You alone, we believe in You, and we place our trust in You and praise You with good.

And we are grateful to You and are not ungrateful, we free ourselves and leave the one who is ungrateful to You.

O Allāh! You alone do we worship and we pray only to You. We bow before You alone and we hasten eagerly towards You. We hope for Your mercy and fear Your punishment, verily Your punishment will fall upon the disbelievers. And may Allāh send salutations upon the Honourable Prophet.

Ṣalāh

Ṣalātul Qaṣr

'Qaṣr' means to make something short. Allāh in His kindness shortens the ṣalah for a person who is travelling.

A person who plans to travel 54.5 miles* (87.7 km) or more away from the boundary of his city will perform qaṣr ṣalāh. A person who intends to stay at the destination for fewer than 15 days will also pray qaṣr ṣalāh there.

Ṣalātul Qaṣr 

Fajr: 2 farḍ (as normal)

Ẓuhr: 2 farḍ

'Aṣr: 2 farḍ

Maghrib: 3 farḍ (as normal)

'Ishā': 2 farḍ 3 witr

The two sunnah of fajr are very important and should be prayed even when travelling.

*Some 'Ulamā' hold the view that the qaṣr distance is 48 miles (77 km). Whichever opinion one adopts, consistency in practice is essential.

Ṣalāh

Ṣalātul Marīḍ

Ṣalāh is so important in Islām that even if you are unwell or bed-ridden, you still have to perform ṣalāh.

However, Allāh سبحانه وتعالى is very merciful with us. If we are unwell or have an illness, ṣalāh can be performed in a different posture.

As long as we can stand and perform ṣalāh, we are not allowed to sit and perform ṣalāh. A person who cannot stand at all should sit down on the floor and perform ṣalāh. They will perform rukū' by lowering their head and perform sajdah as usual.

A person who cannot do sajdah can perform ṣalāh sitting down. They will make gestures with their head for rukū' and sajdah in such a manner that the gestures for sajdah are lower than those used in rukū'.

Only when a person cannot perform sajdah and it is very difficult and painful for them to sit on the floor, they would be allowed to sit on a chair. Otherwise, one should sit on the floor and perform ṣalāh.

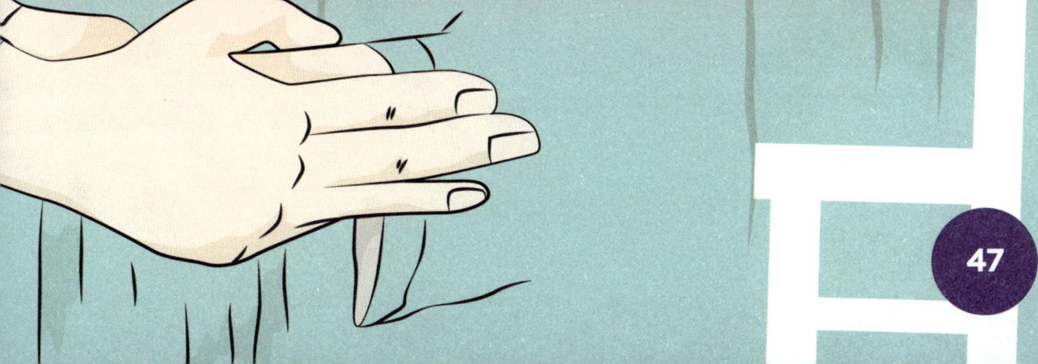

Aḥādīth

Aḥādīth

Aḥādīth

قَالَ رَسُوْلُ اللهِ صَلَّى اللهُ عَلَيْهِ وَسَلَّمَ

اَلصَّلَاةُ عِمَادُ الدِّيْنِ

اَحِبَّ لِلنَّاسِ مَا تُحِبُّ لِنَفْسِكَ تَكُنْ مُسْلِمًا

قُلْ اٰمَنْتُ بِاللهِ ثُمَّ اسْتَقِمْ

كُنْ فِي الدُّنْيَا كَاَنَّكَ غَرِيْبٌ أَوْ عَابِرُ سَبِيْلٍ

اَلدُّنْيَا سِجْنُ الْمُؤْمِنِ وَجَنَّةُ الْكَافِرِ

اَلدُّعَاءُ سِلَاحُ الْمُؤْمِنِ

مَنْ كَانَ يُؤْمِنُ بِاللهِ وَالْيَوْمِ الْاٰخِرِ فَلْيُكْرِمْ ضَيْفَهُ

لَا يَرْحَمُ اللهُ مَنْ لَّا يَرْحَمُ النَّاسَ

اَلْحَيَاءُ شُعْبَةٌ مِّنَ الْاِيْمَانِ

اَفْضَلُ الدُّعَاءِ اَلْحَمْدُ لِلّٰهِ

Ṣalāh

Aḥādīth

قَالَ رَسُولُ اللهِ صَلَّى اللهُ عَلَيْهِ وَسَلَّمَ

Rasūlullāh صلى الله عليه وسلم said:

اَلصَّلَاةُ عِمَادُ الدِّيْنِ

"Ṣalāh is a pillar of dīn"
(Bayḥaqī)

A building cannot stand without a pillar. Without ṣalāh a person cannot have dīn. Ṣalāh is such a worship that makes us different from other religions. Ṣalāh will be the first thing we will be questioned about on the Day of Judgement.

The people of Jahannam will be asked what led them to Jahannam. The first thing they will say is, "We were not from the people who used to pray ṣalāh."(Qur'ān 74:43)

We can see from all these important points that this is a very important part of our dīn.

Love for Others

قَالَ رَسُولُ اللهِ صَلَّى اللهُ عَلَيْهِ وَسَلَّمَ

Rasūlullāh صلى الله عليه وسلم said:

أَحِبَّ لِلنَّاسِ مَا تُحِبُّ لِنَفْسِكَ تَكُنْ مُسْلِمًا

"Love for people what you love for yourself, (and) you will become a true Muslim." (Tirmidhī)

A true believer is selfless. A true believer is not selfish. They are not greedy and think about others. We like to have good clothes, good food, good games and good friends. Similarly we should want others to have all these good things as well. We can do this by giving them whatever we can.

If you want people to treat you nicely, you should treat them nicely. If you want to eat good food, then when it is time for your friend to come to your house, you should give them good food. We should not wish in our hearts that we get all these nice things while they don't get any. That is not a sign of a believer.

May Allāh سبحانه وتعالى make us like the Companions who always preferred others over themselves, Āmīn.

Steadfastness

Aḥādith

قَالَ رَسُولُ اللهِ صَلَّى اللهُ عَلَيْهِ وَسَلَّمَ

Rasūlullāh صلى الله عليه وسلم said:

قُلْ اٰمَنْتُ بِاللهِ ثُمَّ اسْتَقِمْ

"Say: 'I believe in Allāh,' then stay firm."
(Ṣaḥīḥ Muslim)

Rasūlullāh صلى الله عليه وسلم has told us that once we have said that we believe in Allāh سبحانه وتعالى, we must stay firm upon it and practise upon what Allāh سبحانه وتعالى has told us to do.

Our belief should be deep in our heart. Sometimes Allāh سبحانه وتعالى may test us to see how strong our īmān is by giving us some difficulty. In these times we must not lose our patience, or say things which are disrespectful. However, we should stay firm. The Companions were very firm in their īmān despite all the difficulties they faced.

Allāh سبحانه وتعالى will grant Jannah to those who believed in Him and thereafter stayed firm and strong in their beliefs. Angels will come and meet such people.

Life

قَالَ رَسُولُ اللّٰهِ صَلَّى اللّٰهُ عَلَيْهِ وَسَلَّمَ

Rasūlullāh  said:

كُنْ فِي الدُّنْيَا كَأَنَّكَ غَرِيبٌ أَوْ عَابِرُ سَبِيلٍ

"Stay in this world as though you are a stranger, rather a traveller."
(Ṣaḥīḥ al-Bukhārī)

This world is like a waiting room at a train station. When we are waiting, do we start thinking about decorating the station? Do we start fighting for the best seat at the station? No of course not. Why? Because we know we are soon moving onto a big journey. We make sure our luggage is secure. We check that we have enough food to last us for the journey.

Similarly, we are here in this world for a short while. Rather than worrying so much about our worldly life, we should spend some time checking our good deeds. Do we have sufficient good deeds to make us pass the test in the grave, and the questioning on the Day of Judgement?

This World

قَالَ رَسُولُ اللّٰهِ صَلَّى اللّٰهُ عَلَيْهِ وَسَلَّمَ

Rasūlullāh صلى الله عليه وسلم said:

اَلدُّنْيَا سِجْنُ الْمُؤْمِنِ وَجَنَّةُ الْكَافِرِ

"The world is a prison for a believer and a paradise for a disbeliever."
(Ṣaḥīḥ Muslim)

Paradise is a place where all desires are fulfilled, whereas in a prison, a person cannot have whatever he wants, whenever he wants. Similarly, Rasūlullāh صلى الله عليه وسلم has informed us that in this world, a Muslim cannot have whatever he wants whenever he wants, so it is like a prison. But a disbeliever follows his desires so this world is like paradise for him. A believer will get what he desires in Jannah.

Du'ā'

قَالَ رَسُولُ اللهِ صَلَّى اللهُ عَلَيْهِ وَسَلَّمَ

Rasūlullāh صلى الله عليه وسلم said:

اَلدُّعَاءُ سِلَاحُ الْمُؤْمِنِ

"Du'ā' is the weapon of a believer."
(Ḥākim)

Aḥādīth

Du'ā' is when a person asks and begs from Allāh سبحانه وتعالى. Rasūlullāh صلى الله عليه وسلم has said that "Du'ā' is a weapon of a believer." Just as a weapon protects you from your enemies, similarly du'ā' protects a person.

When a person makes du'ā', he should first praise Allāh سبحانه وتعالى, and then send ṣalawāt (durūd) to Rasūlullāh صلى الله عليه وسلم. Afterwards he should make du'ā' for himself and everyone else. Finally, he should end the du'ā' with durūd and the praise of Allāh سبحانه وتعالى.

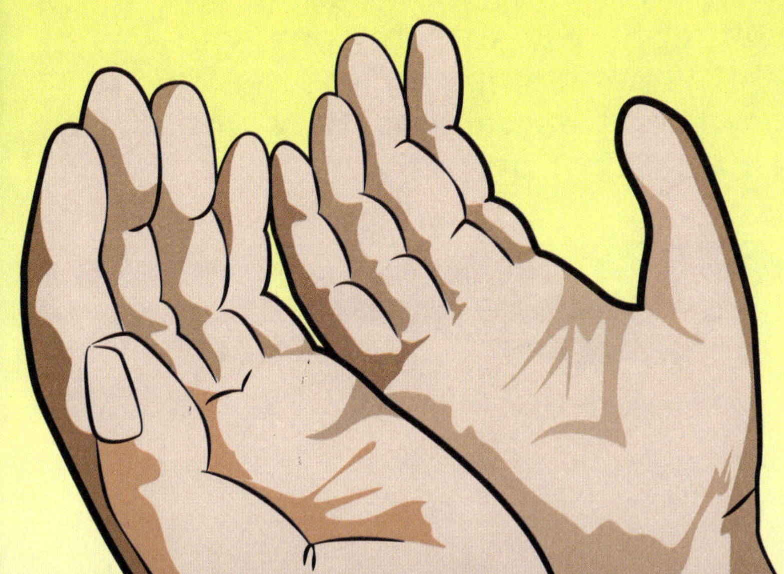

Guests

قَالَ رَسُولُ اللهِ صَلَّى اللهُ عَلَيْهِ وَسَلَّمَ

Rasūlullāh صلى الله عليه وسلم said:

مَنْ كَانَ يُؤْمِنُ بِاللهِ وَالْيَوْمِ الْاٰخِرِ فَلْيُكْرِمْ ضَيْفَهُ

"Whoever believes in Allāh and the Last Day should honour his guest!" (Ṣaḥīḥ al-Bukhārī)

When someone comes to our house, it is good manners to treat them nicely. Honouring the guest was very common with the Ṣaḥābah: they would go hungry at times and ensure their guest was well fed.

One day, a Companion took a guest home. His wife said they only had enough food for the children. The husband told his wife to make the children sleep and prepare the food for their guest.

When the food was put on the table they put the light out and made gestures as if they were eating. The guest did not know that he was the only one who was eating. Subḥānallāh! What an amazing lesson for us to learn from the lives of the Companions: they would stay hungry and let their guest eat properly.

Mercy

قَالَ رَسُولُ اللهِ صَلَّى اللهُ عَلَيْهِ وَسَلَّمَ

Rasūlullāh صلى الله عليه وسلم said:

لَا يَرْحَمُ اللهُ مَنْ لَّا يَرْحَمُ النَّاسَ

"Allāh does not show mercy to the one who does not show mercy to people!"
(Ṣaḥīḥ al-Bukhārī)

Mercy is an act of kindness; being nice to another being. When you are nice, kind, and merciful to one of Allāh سبحانه وتعالى's creation, then Allāh سبحانه وتعالى will be kind to you. But if you do not show them kindness, and instead hurt them, then Allāh سبحانه وتعالى will not have mercy on you. If Allāh سبحانه وتعالى takes His mercy away from a person then who can save him?

Do you remember the story of the lady who was kind to the thirsty dog? Do you recall how Allāh سبحانه وتعالى forgave all her sins? May Allāh سبحانه وتعالى keep us in His mercy.

Āmīn

Modesty

Aḥādīth

قَالَ رَسُولُ اللهِ صَلَّى اللهُ عَلَيْهِ وَسَلَّمَ

Rasūlullāh صلى الله عليه وسلم said:

اَلْحَيَاءُ شُعْبَةٌ مِّنَ الْإِيمَانِ

"Modesty is part of īmān."
(Ṣaḥīḥ al-Bukhārī)

In another ḥadīth, Rasūlullāh صلى الله عليه وسلم said that "If you do not have modesty then do as you please."
(Ṣaḥīḥ al-Bukhārī)

Modesty stops us from doing evil. We must not be immodest, instead we should have modesty in all aspects of our lives.

In our clothing we should ensure that the clothes do not show the body parts which are not allowed to be seen by strangers.

In our behaviour we must be modest by showing good manners.

In our speech we must show modesty by saying what is good and truthful. We must not swear or speak about rude things.

Shukr

قَالَ رَسُولُ اللهِ صَلَّى اللهُ عَلَيْهِ وَسَلَّمَ

Rasūlullāh صلى الله عليه وسلم said:

أَفْضَلُ الدُّعَاءِ الْحَمْدُ لِلّٰهِ

"The best du'ā' is Alḥamdulillāh."
(Tirmidhī)

Allāh سبحانه وتعالى has blessed us with so much. He informs us in the Qur'ān that if we thank Him, He will give us more. Our Beloved Messenger Muḥammad صلى الله عليه وسلم has informed us of the best du'ā'. Through du'ā' we ask Allāh سبحانه وتعالى for different things we want, but if we keep thanking Him then automatically we will get more and more, so it is truly the best du'ā'.

Alḥamdulillāh!

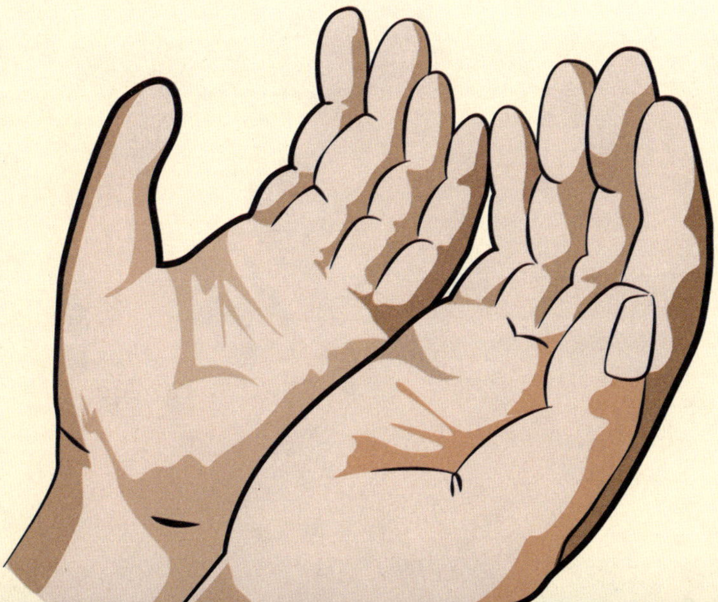

Sīrah

Learning Objectives

Sīrah

At the end of this unit pupils should be able to:

- Explain the reasons for the hijrah to Abyssinia.
- Describe the events that lead to the two great warriors accepting Islām.
- Discuss the boycott and explain how it ended.

- Indicate the reasons why the year was known as the Year of Sadness and what led to the journey of Ṭā'if.
- Differentiate between al-Isrā' and al-Mi'rāj.

- Illustrate the key events of al-Mi'rāj.

Sīrah so far...

Before our Beloved Prophet Muḥammad صلى الله عليه وسلم was made a messenger, he used to feel the pain of the people around him and would think of ways to help them.

He began spending time in the Cave of Ḥirā' thinking about Allāh سبحانه وتعالى. It was here that the Angel Jibra'īl appeared and brought the first verses from Allāh سبحانه وتعالى, whilst the Prophet صلى الله عليه وسلم was forty years old. When the cousin of Khadījah رضي الله عنها, Waraqah, heard about this, he instantly recognised that this was the same angel that had come to Mūsā عليه السلام.

The first person to accept Islām was his beloved wife Khadījah رضي الله عنها. Thereafter, it was Abū Bakr رضي الله عنه, followed by a number of others. Many of the people of Makkah were not happy or prepared to hear his message and began hurting those who believed in the one Allāh. They were reluctant to follow the pure teachings of our Beloved Messenger Muḥammad صلى الله عليه وسلم, and some became aggressive and even spiteful.

Migration to Abyssinia

Sīrah

Slowly the persecution grew worse and by the middle of the fifth year of prophethood, the situation was no longer tolerable. The Messenger صلى الله عليه وسلم gave permission to his Companions to migrate.

A number of the Companions migrated to Abyssinia where the Christian king, Najāshī, was known to be a fair and compassionate ruler.

The first group of Muslims to migrate consisted of twelve men and four women. Among them were 'Uthmān ibn 'Affān رضي الله عنه and his wife Ruqayyah رضي الله عنها, the daughter of the Messenger صلى الله عليه وسلم.

They arrived in Abyssinia and stayed for a few months when they were misinformed that the Quraysh had embraced Islām. They quickly returned only to find that the situation was the same.

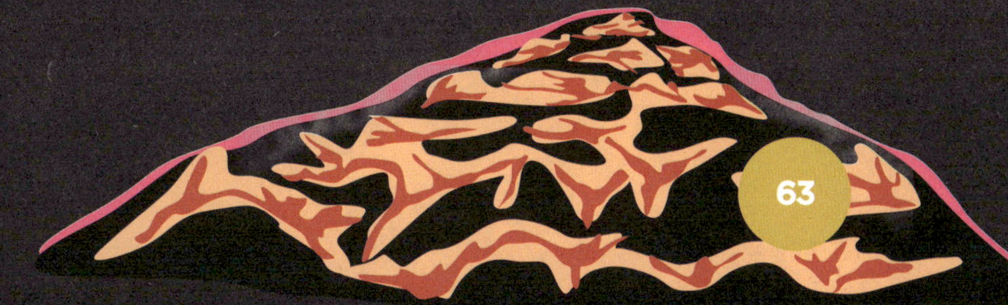

Migration to Abyssinia

The persecution of the Muslims had been stepped up, resulting in severe beatings and ill treatment. Rasūlullāh صلى الله عليه وسلم saw no way out except to give permission to the suffering Muslims to migrate to Abyssinia for a second time. This group consisted of eighty-three men and eighteen women.

The Quraysh followed the Muslims to Abyssinia and requested the King to return the Muslims to them.

It was at this point that a Companion of the Messenger صلى الله عليه وسلم, Ja'far ibn Abī Ṭālib رضي الله عنه, spoke in front of the King.

Migration to Abyssinia

He told him what darkness and evil their lives had been filled with, and how the weak were troubled by the strong until "Allāh sent to us a Messenger from Him with guidance and light. So, we followed and obeyed him until our own community began to hate and hurt us. Our Messenger instructed us to come to your country for safety."

Thereafter Ja'far رضي الله عنه recited the first few verses of Sūrah Maryam, causing everyone to cry. Najāshī told the Quraysh to leave and said that he would never give such people away.

Dear children, always remember that if Allāh سبحانه وتعالى is on your side, then nothing in this world can ever harm you: even if everyone tries to hurt you, Allāh سبحانه وتعالى will always save you.

Two Great Warriors Accept Islām

A turning point to the torture came when two men, who were known and respected for their strength and courage, became Muslims. The first was Ḥamzah ibn 'Abdul Muṭṭalib رضي الله عنه, one of the Prophet's uncles, and the second was 'Umar ibn al-Khaṭṭāb رضي الله عنه.

Abū Jahal spoke rudely to the Messenger صلى الله عليه وسلم in front of the Ka'bah. When Ḥamzah رضي الله عنه heard about Abū Jahal's disgusting behaviour, he was angered and at once went to the compound of the Ka'bah where the chiefs of Makkah were seated. It was here that he openly declared his acceptance of Islām and said that "If anybody ever hurts the Messenger صلى الله عليه وسلم through his tongue or hands, they will have me to face!"

Shortly afterwards, 'Umar ibn al-Khaṭṭāb رضي الله عنه, who had previously been against Islām, accepted Islām. He left home one day with only one thing on his mind: to finish the Messenger صلى الله عليه وسلم.

On his way, he met a friend who informed him that his own sister and brother-in-law had both accepted Islām. Enraged, he set out for his sister's house.

Two Great Warriors Accept Islām

Upon reaching the house, he heard someone reciting the Qur'ān. He burst into the house and started to beat his sister and brother-in-law. He lashed out at them, but they said: "You may beat us but we will not abandon Islām!"

He realised they were not going to back down. He then asked them to show him the verses that they had been reading. His sister insisted that he wash first: these were pure words and had to be treated with respect. When he had become clean, he picked up the pages of the scripture and began to read. It happened to be Sūrah Ṭā Hā (Sūrah 20). By the time he got to the 14th verse, he was a changed man. "Point me in the direction of Muḥammad," now escaped his lips softly. He was taken to the house of Arqam, and it was there that he embraced Islām.

Dear children, we must never look at anyone in a bad way. If Allāh سبحانه وتعالى decides to change anyone, then no matter how bad they may be, Allāh سبحانه وتعالى can change them.

A Different Way

Sīrah

When the disbelievers saw that these two great men had accepted Islām, they realised that hurting the Muslims was of no use. Now they decided to try a different way with the Messenger Muḥammad صلى الله عليه وسلم.

They sent 'Utbah ibn Rabī'ah with tempting bribes to the Messenger صلى الله عليه وسلم. Yet for all his experience and skill, 'Utbah could not get the Messenger صلى الله عليه وسلم to sway. The Messenger صلى الله عليه وسلم recited some verses of Sūrah Fuṣṣilat (Sūrah 41) before him and then said, "You have now heard, O Abal-Walīd, it is now between you and it." 'Utbah left having made no victories.

He told the leaders that the message was not poetry, magic, or the words of fortune-tellers. "Obey me, O people of Quraysh, and let me bear the results of what I tell you." He then advised, "leave this man and what he is doing." This was not what they had expected from such a person.

The Qur'ān is such an amazing book granted to us by Allāh سبحانه وتعالى. We should try and read the Qur'ān every day. Even if we read one page per day, we shall start to become closer to Allāh سبحانه وتعالى until we become His very close friend.

The Boycott

When the disbelievers saw and understood that their persecution and ill treatment had not moved the Muslims away from their religion, they decided on a final try: to totally boycott the tribes of Banū Hāshim and Banū Muṭṭalib.

The disbelievers wrote a set of rules and moved the two tribes out of Makkah, making them settle in a narrow valley known today as Shi'b Abī Ṭālib. No one from Makkah was allowed to speak, mix, buy, sell, or marry within the two tribes until they decided to hand over the Messenger صلى الله عليه وسلم.

This terrible boycott lasted for three years. Afterwards Allāh سبحانه وتعالى sent white ants to eat away the set of rules which were hung on the Ka'bah. Finally, the boycott had ended, the tribes were once again free.

The Year of Sadness

Sīrah

Six months after the end of the boycott, the dear old uncle of the Messenger صلى الله عليه وسلم, Abū Ṭālib, who had withstood much trouble from the Quraysh, but not given up his nephew's side, passed away. Despite all of his support for the Messenger صلى الله عليه وسلم, he did not accept Islām.

A few months after that, the beloved and courageous wife Khadījah رضي الله عنها passed away too. She had been with the Messenger صلى الله عليه وسلم from the beginning, having shared with him the trials and tribulations. She had been a pillar of strength for him. She was sixty-five years old when she passed away.

After the death of Abū Ṭālib, the disbelievers increased their torture and oppression.

The Journey to Ṭā'if

The Messenger صلى الله عليه وسلم decided to take his message outside Makkah. He chose a town not far away called Ṭā'if. The Messenger صلى الله عليه وسلم arrived with great hope, but the leaders did not want to hear what he had to say; they turned a deaf ear to his message.

He stayed for ten days, inviting the leaders, one after the other, but none paid heed to his great message.

Soon they ordered the local people to make fun of him and pelt him with stones. The Beloved Messenger صلى الله عليه وسلم was pelted all the way out of Ṭā'if. Blood flowed from all parts of his body. The Messenger صلى الله عليه وسلم returned to Makkah disheartened and sad.

The Journey to Ṭā'if

Our Beloved Messenger صلى الله عليه وسلم recalling this incident said: "...I departed, overwhelmed with excessive sorrow, and proceeded on, and could not rest till I found myself at 'Qarn ath-Tha'ālib' where I lifted my head towards the sky to see a cloud shading me unexpectedly. I looked up and saw Jibra'īl in it. He called me saying, 'Allāh has heard your people's words to you, and what they have replied back with, Allāh has sent the Angel of the Mountains to you so that you may order him to do whatever you wish to these people.'

The Angel of the Mountains called and greeted me, and then said, 'O Muhammad! Order what you wish. If you like, I will let two mountains fall on them.' The Prophet صلى الله عليه وسلم said, 'No but I hope that Allāh will let them have children who will worship Allāh Alone, and will worship none besides Him.'" (Ṣaḥīḥ al-Bukhārī)

Dear children, look at the last three chapters carefully. The Messenger صلى الله عليه وسلم went through so much pain, trouble, and grief. Did he give up his mission? No. He continued firmly.

We must never give up when we are doing something good, no matter what people say or do to us. We must stay strong just like the Beloved Messenger صلى الله عليه وسلم.

Inviting the Arab Tribes

The Messenger صلى الله عليه وسلم returned to Makkah during the month of Ḥajj. He took this opportunity to invite the different Arab tribes, as well as individuals, who gathered for the sacred pilgrimage.

It was during this season of pilgrimage in the eleventh year of Prophethood, that the call of Islām was answered by a group of people from Yathrib (Madīnah). The Messenger صلى الله عليه وسلم would meet the different tribes carefully in order not to attract the attention of the Quraysh.

This group consisted of six people from the tribe of Khazraj. They had always heard the Jews talk of the final Prophet. To meet this man who proclaimed to be the final Prophet was a wonderful achievement for them. They listened to the Prophet's message enthusiastically and quickly embraced Islām, promising to take this message back with them and invite as many people as possible.

Al-Isrā' and Al-Mi'rāj

Sīrah

Allāh سبحانه وتعالى the Most High stated in the Qur'ān:

"Glorified is He who carried His servant by night from the blessed masjid (of Makkah) to the furthest masjid (of Jerusalem, Masjid al Aqṣā), the surroundings of which We have blessed, that We might show him some of Our signs. Surely He, only He, is the All-Hearing, the All-Seeing." (Qur'ān 17:1)

In the early days of Islām, Allāh سبحانه وتعالى gave the Messenger صلى الله عليه وسلم such miracles, that they even surprised the disbelievers.

A miracle is an extraordinary thing that humans cannot do. Miracles are given by Allāh سبحانه وتعالى to His prophets as a sign for the people.

Al-Isrā' and Al-Mi'rāj

Sīrah

One of these miracles is an event in two parts: Isrā' and Mi'rāj. They took place together in one instant, during one blessed night.

- Isrā', or the Night Journey, is the Prophet صلى الله عليه وسلم's journey from Makkah to Bayt al-Maqdis in Jerusalem. In those days, this journey normally took two months.

- Mi'rāj, or the Ascent, is the Prophet صلى الله عليه وسلم's journey from Bayt al-Maqdis up through to the High Heavens and beyond Sidrah al-Muntahā, (the furthest point of the Heavens). It is where Allāh سبحانه وتعالى revealed to him what He willed, before returning the Messenger صلى الله عليه وسلم back to Bayt al-Maqdis. The miracle of Mi'rāj is a marvellous event during which the Messenger صلى الله عليه وسلم was able to experience something that no other prophet or messenger before him ever had.

Al-Isrā' and Al-Mi'rāj

Sirah

Through the miracle of Isrā' and Mi'rāj, the Messenger صلى الله عليه وسلم was comforted by Allāh سبحانه وتعالى and shown his real status in the Heavens, even though people did not truly recognise the Messenger صلى الله عليه وسلم's status in the world.

We must remember that after hardship, pain, and suffering, always comes comfort, ease and happiness.

So, we must never lose hope and we must keep going!

"Verily, along with the hardship there is ease."
(Qur'ān 94:6)

The Actual Event

The Messenger صلى الله عليه وسلم was sleeping by the Ka'bah one night when Jibra'īl عليه السلام came with a beautiful white animal, larger than a donkey, but smaller than a horse: a horse with wings. This was the amazing creature known as Burāq. Before the Messenger صلى الله عليه وسلم, some other prophets had also ridden the Burāq. When the Messenger صلى الله عليه وسلم intended to mount, it began to shy away. Jibra'īl عليه السلام called out "O Burāq! Why is it so? By Allāh سبحانه وتعالى, no one more honourable than him in Allāh سبحانه وتعالى's sight has ridden you before."

The Burāq was tremendously swift and its movement created no discomfort. Each step of his was as far as the eye could see. The Beloved Messenger صلى الله عليه وسلم and Jibra'īl عليه السلام together headed for Bayt al-Maqdis, also referred to as al-Masjid al-Aqṣā, the furthest masjid, whose surroundings Allāh سبحانه وتعالى had blessed.

The Actual Event

There were many sights en route. They came across a beautiful woman adorned with every item of beauty. Her sleeves were rolled up and she called, "O Muḥammad! Look towards me!" The Messenger صلى الله عليه وسلم did not turn towards her but stared straight ahead. Jibra'īl عليه السلام asked him if he had heard something and the Messenger صلى الله عليه وسلم replied that he had. Jibra'īl عليه السلام disclosed to the Messenger صلى الله عليه وسلم that the woman was the world, "And if you had stopped for her then your ummah would have preferred the world to the hereafter." Thereafter, Jibra'īl عليه السلام presented the Messenger صلى الله عليه وسلم with two vessels: one with wine and the other with milk, and asked him to choose one. He rejected the wine and drank the milk.

The Actual Event

Jibra'īl عليه السلام said "You are guided to nature. If you had taken wine then you and your ummah would have gone astray." The Messenger صلى الله عليه وسلم responded with, "Allāhu Akbar!"- Allāh سبحانه وتعالى is the greatest.

Then they landed at Bayt al-Maqdis, tied the Burāq at the gate, and the Messenger صلى الله عليه وسلم found a vast assembly of people waiting for him. They were all his fellow prophets and messengers of the past whom he was to lead in two rak'āt of ṣalāh.

The Events on the Night of Mi'rāj

A staircase was presented to the Messenger صلى الله عليه وسلم, the like of which no living creature has ever seen. He ascended the staircase until reaching the First Heaven. There Jibra'īl عليه السلام asked the angel to open the gate. The angel inquired, "Who is with you?" Jibra'īl عليه السلام replied "It is Muḥammad صلى الله عليه وسلم." The angel asked, "Has he been called?" Jibra'īl عليه السلام answered "Yes." The gate was opened. Upon entering, the Messenger صلى الله عليه وسلم saw a perfectly created man who was surrounded by souls. When he would look towards those on his right hand side he would smile. When he looked towards those to his left, he would weep. The Messenger صلى الله عليه وسلم asked regarding the man and the souls. Jibra'īl عليه السلام answered, "The perfect man is your father Ādam عليه السلام, and the souls are his offspring. To the right are those deserving of Paradise and those to the left are those deserving of the fire of Hell."

The Prophet صلى الله عليه وسلم made salām to him and Ādam عليه السلام welcomed the Beloved Messenger صلى الله عليه وسلم saying, "Pious son and pious prophet, welcome!"

From the Second Heaven to the Seventh Heaven

Jibra'īl عليه السلام then led the Messenger صلى الله عليه وسلم to the Second Heaven where the gate was opened for them as before. The angel at the gate asked the same question, and the same answers were given. The angels then welcomed the Beloved Messenger Muḥammad صلى الله عليه وسلم. Inside he found two young men whom Jibra'īl introduced as 'Īsā ibn Maryam عليه السلام and Yaḥyā ibn Zakariyyā عليهما السلام. The Prophet صلى الله عليه وسلم greeted them with salām, and they greeted the Messenger صلى الله عليه وسلم and said, "Pious prophet and pious brother, welcome!"

Then Jibra'īl عليه السلام took him to the Third Heaven and had its gates opened; the same questions were asked before the admission was granted. There he found a man who was exceptionally beautiful whom Jibra'īl عليه السلام introduced as the Prophet Yūsuf عليه السلام. He offered him salām and Yūsuf عليه السلام greeted him with, "Pious prophet and pious brother, welcome!"

From the Second Heaven to the Seventh Heaven

In the Fourth Heaven, the Messenger صلى الله عليه وسلم met a dignified looking man, whom Jibra'īl عليه السلام said was the Prophet Idrīs عليه السلام. At the Fifth Heaven the Prophet صلى الله عليه وسلم saw a man who was surrounded by a group of people, and was informed that the prophet was Hārūn ibn 'Imrān عليه السلام and the people were the Banū Isrā'īl.

While at the Sixth Heaven the Prophet صلى الله عليه وسلم met a man who he was informed was Mūsā ibn 'Imrān عليه السلام.

Jibra'īl then took the Messenger صلى الله عليه وسلم to the Seventh Heaven where he saw al-Bayt al-Ma'mūr – a house similar to the Ka'bah on earth. There was a beautiful man there who was reclining against al-Bayt al-Ma'mūr. The Messenger صلى الله عليه وسلم was told, "He is your father Ibrāhīm". Allāh's Messenger صلى الله عليه وسلم offered him salām and he responded with, "Pious son and pious prophet, welcome!"

The Gift of Ṣalāh

The Messenger صلى الله عليه وسلم was told that he was to proceed beyond the Lote Tree of the Furthest Region, the Sidrah al-Muntahā, alone; Jibra'īl عليه السلام could go no further. He then went into the Divine Presence of Allāh سبحانه وتعالى. Allāh سبحانه وتعالى ordained fifty prayers a day for the believers to observe. On his way back through the seven heavens, the Messenger صلى الله عليه وسلم again saw Mūsā عليه السلام who asked him how many prayers the Muslims had been instructed to perform. When the Messenger صلى الله عليه وسلم told him fifty, Mūsā عليه السلام instructed him, "Your people are weak. They will find it difficult to pray so many times each day. Go back to your Lord and ask him to reduce the number." The Messenger صلى الله عليه وسلم returned and Allāh سبحانه وتعالى reduced the number by five. When the Messenger صلى الله عليه وسلم passed by him again, Mūsā عليه السلام asked the same question, and again he advised the Messenger صلى الله عليه وسلم to go back. This went on until Allāh سبحانه وتعالى reduced the number to five. Mūsā عليه السلام again advised the Messenger صلى الله عليه وسلم to return but this time he refused saying, "I have asked my Lord to reduce the number until I am ashamed. I will not ask again."

The Gift of Ṣalāh

Dear children, look how kind Allāh سبحانه وتعالى is. From fifty prayers a day He cut it down to only five, and shall give the reward of fifty. We must try to pray all our ṣalāh everyday to please Allāh سبحانه وتعالى.

Al-Isrā' and Al-Mi'rāj

Sīrah

The next morning upon his return, he told the Quraysh about his extraordinary journey. Most of them refused to believe that this miraculous journey was possible. They laughed at the story and sneered at the Muslims, "Look what your Prophet صلى الله عليه وسلم now says!" Abū Jahl was amazed and ran to Abū Bakr رضي الله عنه with the news. Abū Bakr Aṣ-Ṣiddīq رضي الله عنه's immediate response was, "If Muḥammad صلى الله عليه وسلم has said so, then it is true."

Tārīkh

Learning Objectives

Tārīkh

At the end of this unit pupils should be able to:

- Outline the events in the early life of Ibrāhīm عليه السلام.

- Recall the incident with the idols which led the people to throw Ibrāhīm عليه السلام into the fire.

- Describe the events that brought about the water of Zamzam.

- Explain the dream of Ibrāhīm عليه السلام regarding the sacrifice of Ismā'īl عليه السلام.
- Explain how the Ka'bah was built.

Ibrāhīm عليه السلام

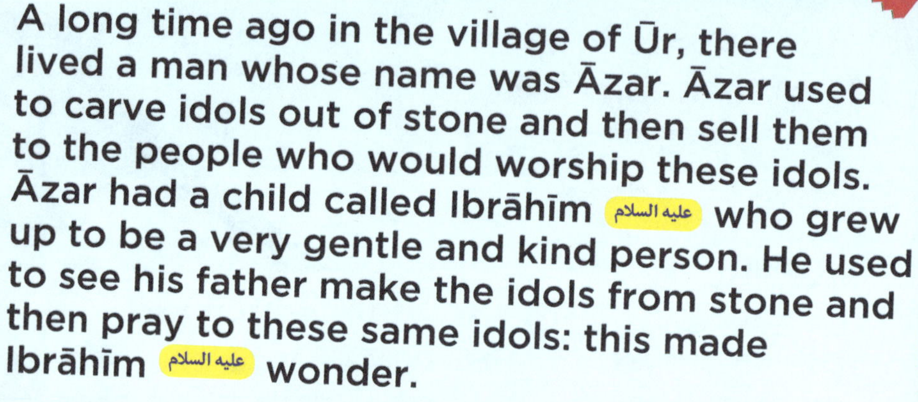

A long time ago in the village of Ūr, there lived a man whose name was Āzar. Āzar used to carve idols out of stone and then sell them to the people who would worship these idols. Āzar had a child called Ibrāhīm عليه السلام who grew up to be a very gentle and kind person. He used to see his father make the idols from stone and then pray to these same idols: this made Ibrāhīm عليه السلام wonder.

Ibrāhīm عليه السلام saw that flies sat on the idols but they did not push the flies away. He saw that people put food out for the idols but no one except mice would eat it.

So Ibrāhīm عليه السلام said to his father, "O my beloved father, why do you worship these stones? These stones cannot speak or hear. They cannot give harm or help." Āzar became angry and did not understand.

Ibrāhīm عليه السلام

In the village there was a huge temple full of idols, which the people would worship. Each year they would celebrate a festival. All the people went to celebrate on this day. One year Ibrāhīm عليه السلام did not go: he wanted to show everyone how wrong they were in worshipping these idols made out of stone.
He went to the large building when no one was there.

Ibrāhīm عليه السلام entered the building and saw the idols. He said, "There is food and drink here, why are you not taking it? Why are you not talking?" Ibrāhīm عليه السلام then took an axe and broke all the idols except the largest one. He then hung the axe on the largest idol's shoulder.

Ibrāhīm 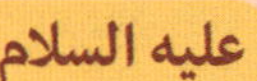

The People Return

When the celebrations finished, the people returned and wanted to pray to the idols. When they came in, they were shocked to see that all of them, except one, lay in pieces! They began asking angrily, "Who has done this to our gods?" (Qur'ān 21:59)

The people said "We have heard a young man talking about them. He is called Ibrāhīm." (Qur'ān 21:60)

They made Ibrāhīm عليه السلام come in front of them and asked him if he had broken the idols. Ibrāhīm عليه السلام explained that the chief idol had done it and asked the people to question the chief idol about the incident.

The people became very confused. 'Then, hanging their heads they reversed their position (and replied to Ibrāhīm عليه السلام) "You already knew that they do not speak." He (Ibrāhīm عليه السلام) said, "Do you then worship, beside Allah, what does not benefit you at all or harm you? (Qur'ān 21:65-66)

Ibrāhīm عليه السلام

The people gathered together and did not know what to do. How should they punish Ibrāhīm عليه السلام for what he had done, they wondered.

"They cried: 'Burn him and stand by your gods...'" (Qur'ān 21:68)

And it was decided. A huge fire was lit. So hot was this fire that if a bird passed over it, it would fall in after being roasted. Ibrāhīm عليه السلام knew his Lord would protect him so he was not scared. Ibrāhīm عليه السلام was thrown into the fire. Allāh سبحانه وتعالى commanded the fire:

"'O fire, be cool and peaceful for Ibrāhīm', and they wished to set a plot for him, but We made them the greater losers. And We rescued him..." (Qur'ān 21:69-70)

Ibrāhīm عليه السلام was not harmed by the fire. When the people saw that they could not harm Ibrāhīm عليه السلام, they became embarrassed and left him.

One night Ibrāhīm عليه السلام looked at the stars and said "This is my Lord," but when the stars vanished he said, "No, this is not my Lord." Then Ibrāhīm عليه السلام saw the moon and said "This is my Lord," but when it too vanished and the morning came he said again, "No, this cannot be my Lord."

Ibrāhīm عليه السلام

Tārīkh

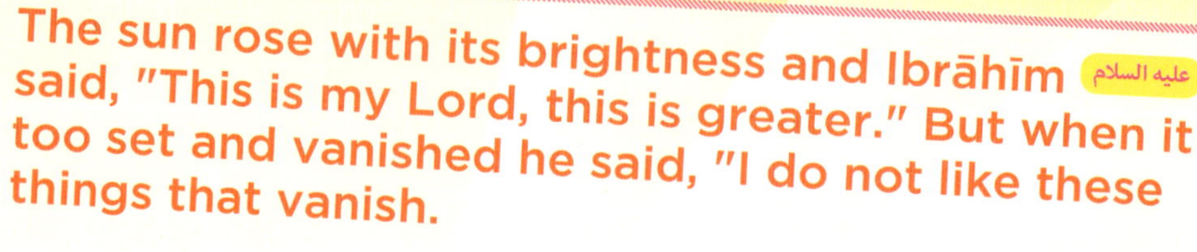

The sun rose with its brightness and Ibrāhīm عليه السلام said, "This is my Lord, this is greater." But when it too set and vanished he said, "I do not like these things that vanish.

"My Lord is Allāh سبحانه وتعالى. Allāh سبحانه وتعالى is everlasting and does not die, Allāh سبحانه وتعالى is the Almighty and nothing can overcome Him. The stars are weak as they are overcome by the moon, the moon is weak as it is overcome by the sun, and the sun is weak as it is overcome by darkness."

"Allāh سبحانه وتعالى is never overpowered, he is always there. He is the Lord of the stars, the moon, the sun, and everything else. He is the Lord of the worlds."

Ibrāhīm عليه السلام was chosen as a messenger. He invited his people and told them about Allāh سبحانه وتعالى and said, "My Allāh سبحانه وتعالى is the One who created and guided me, He is the One who feeds and gives me drink and when I am sick He is the One who cures me." (Qur'ān 26:78-80)

The idols could not do any of these things.

Ibrāhīm عليه السلام

In Front of the King

The king of the area, whose name was Namrūd, heard about Ibrāhīm عليه السلام and that he did not bow down to anyone. Namrūd was a very evil king and used to trouble his people.

He began debating with Ibrāhīm عليه السلام.

He was arrogant and proud because he had the kingdom.

When Ibrāhīm عليه السلام said to him: "My Lord is He Who gives life and causes death," he answered: "I give life and cause death."

He then called two prisoners, freed one of them, and killed the other. He said, "Look I give life and death." Ibrāhīm عليه السلام saw that Namrūd did not understand his words. So, he responded:

"...'Allāh causes the sun to rise in the East, so you should try to cause it to come up from the West.' So the disbeliever was speechless..." (Qur'ān 2:258)

Ibrāhīm عليه السلام

To Makkah

Ibrāhīm عليه السلام then visited his father again to invite him to Allāh سبحانه وتعالى. When his father did not listen, Ibrāhīm عليه السلام decided to leave the city and call other people to Allāh سبحانه وتعالى.

Ibrāhīm عليه السلام had two wives: Sārah and Hājar. He also had two sons: Ismā'īl عليه السلام (son of Hājar) and Isḥāq عليه السلام (son of Sārah).

Allāh سبحانه وتعالى commanded Ibrāhīm عليه السلام to travel to a barren land called Makkah with his wife Hājar and son Ismā'īl عليه السلام. Makkah was an empty desert at that time. There wasn't a single plant or tree in Makkah, and there was no water either.

When Ibrāhīm عليه السلام reached Makkah, Allāh سبحانه وتعالى commanded him to leave his wife and son there and return back. When he was leaving, his wife asked him, "Are you leaving us here alone? Did Allāh سبحانه وتعالى command you to?" Ibrāhīm عليه السلام nodded his head. Hājar replied, "Then He will protect us."

Ibrāhīm عليه السلام

Zamzam

The food and water that Hājar had brought with her was soon finished. Ismā'īl عليه السلام began feeling thirsty so Hājar went to search for water.

There were two mountains in Makkah: Ṣafā and Marwah. Hājar went between these two mountains seven times, trying to see if she could see anyone who could help, or if she could see any sign of water.

Allāh سبحانه وتعالى sent help to Hājar and her son.

Whilst Ismā'īl عليه السلام was on the sand, an angel appeared and hit the ground and immediately water spurted out. Hājar and Ismā'īl thanked Allāh سبحانه وتعالى for this blessing. This water was the blessed water of Zamzam.

Zamzam is still flowing in the city of Makkah. Millions of people drink from it and it has never finished. Subḥānallāh! Zamzam is a miracle.

Ibrāhīm عليه السلام

Tārīkh

The Sacrifice

Ibrāhīm عليه السلام returned to Makkah after a while. When he came back, Allāh سبحانه وتعالى wanted to test Ibrāhīm عليه السلام again.

Ibrāhīm عليه السلام saw a dream in which he was sacrificing his son Ismā'īl عليه السلام. A prophet's dream is a revelation from Allāh سبحانه وتعالى.

He mentioned the dream to his son who said, "Dear father, do as you have been ordered, you shall find me of the patient ones."
(Qur'ān 37:102)

Ibrāhīm عليه السلام took Ismā'īl عليه السلام to slaughter him. On the way Shayṭān tried to make him change his mind. Ibrāhīm عليه السلام pelted the Shayṭān at three different places.

When Ibrāhīm عليه السلام reached the place, he laid Ismā'īl عليه السلام down, but the knife would not cut. Allāh سبحانه وتعالى wanted to see if Ibrāhīm عليه السلام would do what Allāh had commanded him to do. The test was over and Ibrāhīm عليه السلام had passed the test. Allāh سبحانه وتعالى sent a ram from Jannah and told Ibrāhīm عليه السلام to sacrifice the ram instead.

Ibrāhīm 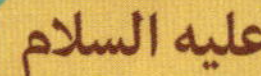

Building the Ka'bah

Allāh سبحانه وتعالى loved the action of Ibrāhīm عليه السلام so much that he ordered all the Muslims to make a sacrifice of an animal for Allāh سبحانه وتعالى every year.

Because of this, Muslims sacrifice an animal at the time of 'Īd al-Aḍḥā.

Allāh سبحانه وتعالى then commanded Ibrāhīm عليه السلام and Ismā'īl عليه السلام to build a house for His worship. So they began building a house, built specially for the worship of Allāh سبحانه وتعالى. This house was called the Ka'bah. It became the direction to which all Muslims face when performing ṣalāh. This direction is known as the 'qiblah.'

Allāh سبحانه وتعالى commanded Ibrāhīm عليه السلام to call people to come and visit the house for pilgrimage. This is farḍ once in a lifetime on every Muslim who is able to and can afford the journey. This is called Ḥajj.

With his other son Isḥāq عليه السلام, Ibrāhīm عليه السلام built another place of worship in Jerusalem called Masjid Al-Aqṣā.

Isḥāq عليه السلام had a son who was called Ya'qūb who was chosen to be a prophet. Ya'qūb عليه السلام had twelve sons. One of the sons was Yūsuf عليه السلام.

‘Aqā’id

Learning Objectives

'Aqā'id

At the end of this unit pupils should be able to:

Classify the two types of messengers and their attributes.

List the prophets mentioned in the Qur'ān.

Explain the Last Day.

Distinguish between minor and major signs of the Last Day.

Messengers

Allāh سبحانه وتعالى created us to worship Him and obey His commands. If we listen to Him, He will reward us with Jannah. We were told about this by the messengers and prophets sent by Allāh سبحانه وتعالى.

Allāh سبحانه وتعالى, the Almighty Creator, selected people at different times and gave them a message through the Angel Jibra'īl.

Allāh سبحانه وتعالى told them to tell their people what Allāh سبحانه وتعالى wanted them to do in this world.

The messengers and prophets were all human.

They were chosen by Allāh سبحانه وتعالى.

They were free from sin.

Allāh سبحانه وتعالى granted them many miracles to prove to the people that they were truly sent by Allāh سبحانه وتعالى to deliver His message.

They always spoke the truth.

Messengers

All the messengers and prophets came with the same main message, which was to believe in one Allāh سبحانه وتعالى and not associate any partners with Him.

The prophets and messengers taught the people how to lead their lives as good human beings.

Some people believed in the message, whilst others rejected and disbelieved it.

Many of those that rejected this message were destroyed in this world.

Two key terms to remember are:

1. Rasūl: a messenger, who is given a book or a scripture and new laws.
2. Nabī: a prophet, who follows the book and law of the previous messenger.

Every rasūl was a nabī, but not every nabī was a rasūl.

Messengers

The first prophet was Ādam عليه السلام.

The last prophet was our Beloved Messenger Muḥammad صلى الله عليه وسلم.

There will be no more prophets or messengers after Muḥammad صلى الله عليه وسلم; he was the final and last messenger.

Anyone that says he is the prophet after Muḥammad صلى الله عليه وسلم is a liar.

We must believe in all the prophets and messengers sent by Allāh سبحانه وتعالى.

A person rejecting a single prophet cannot be called a Muslim.

A person cannot follow the laws of the previous leader if they are different to the leader of his time. Similarly, we cannot follow the commands of the previous prophets. We must only follow the commands of our Messenger Muḥammad صلى الله عليه وسلم.

Allāh سبحانه وتعالى sent down many messengers and prophets. The Qur'ān mentions 25 of them by name.

Messengers

The 25 prophets mentioned in the Qur'ān are:

1. Ādam عليه السلام
2. Idrīs عليه السلام
3. Nūḥ عليه السلام
4. Hūd عليه السلام
5. Ṣāliḥ عليه السلام
6. Ibrāhīm عليه السلام
7. Lūṭ عليه السلام
8. Ismā'īl عليه السلام
9. Isḥāq عليه السلام
10. Ya'qūb عليه السلام
11. Yūsuf عليه السلام
12. Ayyūb عليه السلام
13. Shu'ayb عليه السلام
14. Mūsā عليه السلام
15. Hārūn عليه السلام
16. Dhul-Kifl عليه السلام
17. Dāwūd عليه السلام
18. Sulaymān عليه السلام
19. Ilyās عليه السلام
20. Al-Yasa' عليه السلام
21. Yūnus عليه السلام
22. Zakariyyā عليه السلام
23. Yaḥyā عليه السلام
24. 'Īsā عليه السلام
25. Muḥammad صلى الله عليه وسلم

We say عليه السلام "'Alayhis salām" after the name of every prophet, which means "Peace be upon him."

We say صلى الله عليه وسلم "Ṣallallāhu 'alayhi wasallam" after our Beloved Messenger صلى الله عليه وسلم's name, and this means "May Allāh send blessings and peace on him."

Messengers

Messengers and prophets were many in number,
Sent down from one God, the Almighty Creator.
From Ādam to Muḥammad, peace be upon them,
Shone in this world, more than diamonds and gems,
Islām is what they taught,
The truth is what they brought,
Each of them was outstanding,
Their qualities were amazing,
They were far above all,
Towards Allāh they did call.
Dāwūd and his voice, it was second to none,
Such a sweet voice, not given to everyone.
Sulaymān and his kingdom, Allāh granted him power,
Jinns and angels, and he had great honour;
These are just examples, of the messengers of Allāh.

All great in status, all beloved to their Creator,
Ibrāhīm, Isḥāq and Ya'qūb, all mentioned in the Qur'ān,
Not forgetting Nūḥ and Dāwūd, Yūsuf and Sulaymān,
Ayyūb, Hārūn and Mūsā, Ismā'īl, Al-Yasa' and 'Īsā,
Yūnus, Lūṭ and Ilyās, Zakariyyā and Yaḥyā,
These are the prophets, the Qur'ān has informed,
Muḥammad was the last,
Now prophethood won't be reformed.

Peace be upon them all.

Qiyāmah (The Day of Judgement)

(The time of) their account has approached for the people, while they are in heedlessness turning away. (Qur'ān 21:1)

A day will come when everything will be destroyed: every standing mountain, every flowing ocean, and every living being will perish and die. Nothing will be left except Allāh سبحانه وتعالى.

After a time, when Allāh سبحانه وتعالى wishes, He will recreate again, and take account of everything we did in this world. This happening is called the Day of Judgement, the Last Day, or Yawmul Qiyāmah.

We as Muslims believe in the occurrence of this day. We know and believe that we will have to answer for the things we have done. Allāh سبحانه وتعالى has given us this life as a test. If we pass this test He will reward us on the Day of Judgement by granting us Jannah. If someone fails in this test, He will punish them by making such a person enter Jahannam.

Qiyāmah (The Day of Judgement)

Before a great event comes there are always signs that point to it coming closer. Similarly, the Day of Judgement is one of the greatest days ever, for it is the Last Day. Our Beloved Messenger Muḥammad صلى الله عليه وسلم very kindly told us of many signs that will come before the Day of Judgement. These signs are split into two, occurring in two stages. Stage one involves the minor signs, whilst stage two contains the major signs.

`Aqā'id

Minor Signs

There are many minor signs that will occur before the major signs. When we see these things happening we should know that we are heading closer to the Day of Judgement. Here are some of the minor signs:

- Modesty decreases.
- People begin to cheat in weighing goods.
- Droughts and famines befall the people.
- Rulers oppress their people.
- People withhold paying their zakāh.
- Disunity becomes common.
- Lots of different groups exist.
- A trust becomes a means of making a profit.
- A man obeys his wife but disobeys his mother.
- A person treats his friends kindly whilst ignoring his father.
- Voices are raised in the masjid.
- The leader of a people is the worst of them.
- Wine is drunk a lot.
- Men wear silk.
- Female singers and musical instruments become popular.
- People begin to curse those that came before them.
- People believe in stars and reject destiny.

Major Signs

- The Mahdi رضي الله عنه.
- The Dajjāl.
- 'Īsā عليه السلام returns.
- Ya'jūj and Ma'jūj.
- Landslides.
- The Smoke.
- Emergence of the Beast from the earth.
- Rising of the sun from the West.
- The Fire.
- The Wind that will take every believer's soul.

Akhlāq

Akhlāq

Learning Objectives

Akhlāq

At the end of this unit pupils should be able to:

Explain the importance in 'thinking good of others.'

Recall the stories on sharing with others.

Emphasise the great status of parents, given by Allāh سبحانه وتعالى and his Prophet صلى الله عليه وسلم.

Justify how the truth can lead to success in this world and the hereafter.

Demonstrate how to say a good word or keep quiet in difficult situations.

Describe how 'ghībah' will cancel out good deeds.

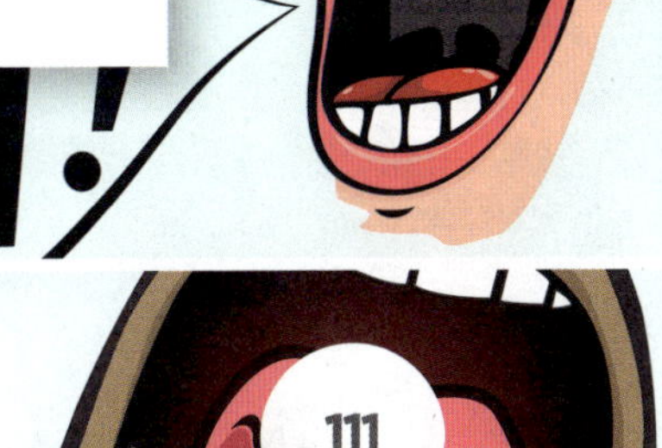

Thinking Good of Others

O you who believe, abstain from much suspicion. Some suspicions are sins. (Qur'ān 49:12)

Our Beloved Messenger Muḥammad صلى الله عليه وسلم said: "Save yourself from suspicion because suspicion is the biggest lie." (Ṣaḥīḥ al-Bukhārī)

He also stated that "Shayṭān circulates in the human being as blood circulates in the body." (Ṣaḥīḥ al-Bukhārī)

Thinking good of others is very important. We must not think badly of people, for only Allāh سبحانه وتعالى knows what is in the hearts of people.

As we can see from the āyah mentioned above: "Some suspicions are sins": this should be enough for a Muslim to stop just by knowing that Allāh سبحانه وتعالى is displeased with him.

Thinking Good of Others

Regret is wishing you hadn't done a particular action in the past. Being suspicious of someone often leads to regret.

Disunity is caused by hatred. When we think badly of people we begin treating them differently: this will in turn lead to disunity. When we are disunited, Allāh سبحانه وتعالى's mercy will move away from us.

Evil/bad thoughts may lead to other major sins. At times we may think bad of a person and then begin to talk about our suspicions to other people: this is the sin of ghībah (backbiting). In trying to find more things about this person, the sin of tajassus (spying) may be committed.

Thinking Good of Others

How can we stop thinking bad about people?

- Think good of other people. This is a positive quality which will keep us happy and away from much harm.
- Find excuses. It has been said "find for your fellow Muslim seventy excuses before you suspect or accuse him of anything."

Here are a couple of examples:

You see someone eating in the month of Ramaḍān when everyone is supposed to be fasting.

Bad thought: "Look at this sinful person: he does not even follow the pillars of Islām."
Good thought: "Maybe this person is very ill and due to medication, he is unable to fast. Let me pray for him."

You knock at a door three times but nobody answers.

Bad thought: "They don't want to let me come in."
Good thought: "They must be busy and didn't hear the knocks."

Thinking Good of Others

There is always a good thought you can have instead of a bad one.

Can you think of more examples?

Worry about yourself

Allāh سبحانه وتعالى will not ask you on the Day of Judgement about other people's private lives. But He will ask you about how you spent your time. Why should we worry whether a person is doing this or not, or why he meets such-and-such a person? We don't have much time! The Angel of Death could arrive at any time to take us to meet our Creator: we should be busy collecting good deeds.

Make Du'ā'

رَبَّنَا اغْفِرْ لَنَا وَلِإِخْوَانِنَا الَّذِينَ سَبَقُونَا بِالْإِيمَانِ وَلَا تَجْعَلْ فِي قُلُوبِنَا غِلًّا لِّلَّذِينَ آمَنُوا رَبَّنَا إِنَّكَ رَءُوفٌ رَّحِيمٌ

Our Lord, forgive us and those of our brothers who preceded us in faith, and do not place in our hearts any hatred against those who believe; Surely, our Lord, You are very kind, very merciful. (Qur'ān 59:10)

Thinking Good of Others

We should make sure we always have good thoughts about our Creator, Allāh سبحانه وتعالى.

Abū Hurayrah رضي الله عنه reports that the Beloved Prophet صلى الله عليه وسلم said that Allāh سبحانه وتعالى stated, "I am as My servant thinks I am.' (Ṣaḥīḥ al-Bukhārī)

If a person sins and wishes to repent to Allāh سبحانه وتعالى, then he should think in his heart that Allāh سبحانه وتعالى will forgive him. One must not think Allāh سبحانه وتعالى will not forgive him, for Allāh سبحانه وتعالى's mercy is greater than anything.

Sometimes Shayṭān makes us think in a bad way so that we stop doing good actions.

Ḥasan al-Baṣri رحمه الله said, "If the Mu'min thinks good of Allāh سبحانه وتعالى, he will continually do good (actions)."

We should always think good of Allāh سبحانه وتعالى in every situation. We should never lose hope.

When we make du'ā' to Allāh سبحانه وتعالى we should be confident that Allāh سبحانه وتعالى will surely answer our prayers.

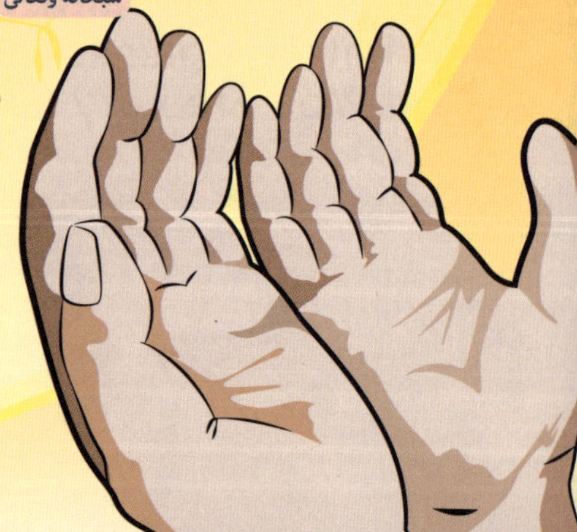

Thinking Good of Others

Allāh سبحانه وتعالى tells us: "When My servants ask you about Me, then (tell them that) I am near. I respond to the call of the caller when he prays to Me; so they should respond to Me, and have faith in Me, so that they may be on the right path." (Qur'ān 2:186)

Sometimes we may not immediately get what we have asked for. This is because Allāh سبحانه وتعالى is so kind: He knows what is good for us. Later in life when we look back at our years, we may see that if Allāh سبحانه وتعالى had given us everything we asked for, we would not have had all those good things that came our way instead.

"It could be that you dislike something, when it is good for you; and it could be that you like something when it is bad for you. Allāh knows and you do not know." (Qur'ān 2:216)

We should never stop asking Allāh 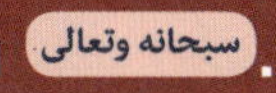.

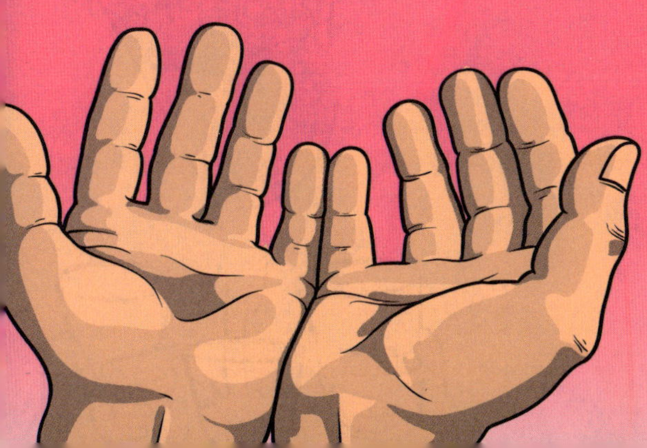

Sharing with Others

"You shall never attain righteousness unless you spend from what you love. Whatsoever you spend, Allāh is fully aware of it." **(Qur'ān 3:92)**

"(They) give preference (to them) over themselves, even though they are in poverty. And those who are saved from the greed of their hearts are the successful." **(Qur'ān 59:9)**

Abū Hurayrah رضي الله عنه reports that the Beloved Messenger صلى الله عليه وسلم said: "...Greed and faith can never co-exist in the human heart." **(Nasa'ī)**

The Messenger of Allāh صلى الله عليه وسلم said that, "...a miser shall not enter Jannah." (Tirmidhī)

Akhlāq

Sharing is indeed caring and has been encouraged by Allāh سبحانه وتعالى in the Qur'ān: if we truly want to become close to Allāh سبحانه وتعالى we should give what we love.

Sharing with Others

The Companions would love sharing with others and they would always prefer other people over themselves. This is what made them special: they were selfless and not selfish.

One day there were three Companions, all of whom were injured and extremely thirsty. A person approached the first Companion with a glass of water but just then he heard the other Companion ask for water: he immediately indicated that the person go to the other Companion.

When he arrived at the second Companion, he too heard the plea of a third Companion, thus he ushered the person to him. When he arrived at the third Companion, he found that he had passed away. Quickly returning to the second Companion he found that he too had passed away. Finally he went back to the first Companion and found that he too had passed away.

All three of the Companions of our Beloved Messenger Muḥammad صلى الله عليه وسلم had sacrificed their thirst for the need of the other; each of them preferred the other over themselves.

Subḥānallāh, what great examples the Companions left for us! May Allāh سبحانه وتعالى be pleased with them all.

Sharing with Others

We must always try to share what we have. It could be something so simple like an apple, but if we share it, Allāh سبحانه وتعالى will love us and this will create love between us all. When we share we are showing good manners.

Remember everything we have been given is from Allāh سبحانه وتعالى. So when we share with others, it is not something of ours that we are sharing, but what actually belongs to Allāh سبحانه وتعالى.

If we share with others, people will share with us.

We can share our food, our sweets, and our books. Sharing takes greed out of a person. Greed grows inside a person and he is never happy: he always wants more and more.

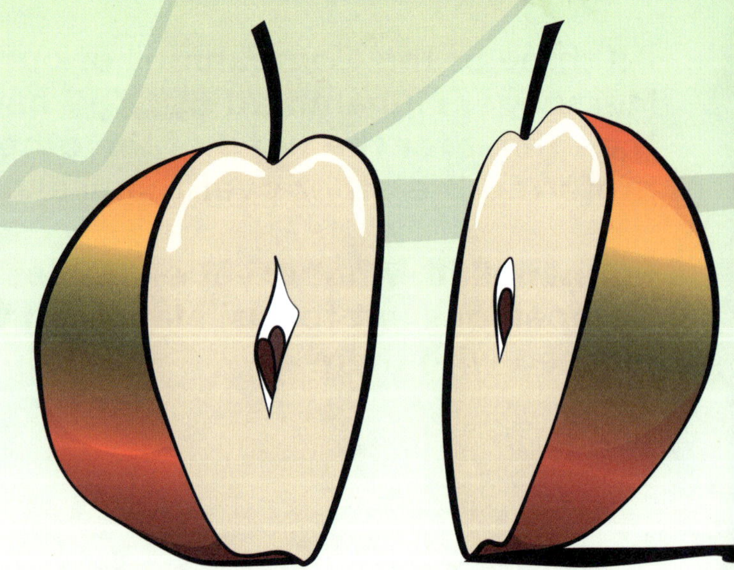

Sharing with Others

Ibn 'Umar رضي الله عنه said "One of the Ṣaḥābah received a goat's head as a present. He thought of a neighbour who had a larger family and was in greater need of it than himself so he presented it to him. This brother, on receipt of the present, thought of a person whom he considered even more deserving than himself, and sent the head to him. It is said that the head changed hands no less than seven times, and at last came back to the original person. (Ṭabarānī)

The Ṣaḥābah indeed preferred others above themselves even though they were in need.

Kindness to Parents

"Your Lord has decreed that you worship none but Him, and do good to parents. If any one of them or both of them reach old age, do not say to them: 'uff' (a word or expression of anger or contempt) and do not scold them, and address them with respectful words, and submit yourself before them in humility out of compassion, and say, 'My Lord, be merciful to them as they have brought me up in my childhood.'

Your Lord knows best what is in your hearts. If you are righteous, then He is Most-Forgiving for those who turn to Him in repentance." (Qur'ān 17:23-25)

Kindness to Parents

Our parents are one of the greatest gifts Allāh سبحانه وتعالى has blessed us with: we can never pay them back for all the things they have done for us.

Allāh سبحانه وتعالى has placed great importance on obedience to parents. He mentioned their rights immediately after His rights. We have been commanded to respect them in the highest way and not to even 'tut' in front of them.

Anas رضي الله عنه reports that the Beloved Messenger صلى الله عليه وسلم had mentioned the major sins and said they are shirk and disobedience to parents. (Ṣaḥīḥ al-Bukhārī)

'Abdullāh ibn 'Umar رضي الله عنه reported that the Messenger of Allāh صلى الله عليه وسلم said that, "Allāh's happiness is in the father's happiness and Allāh's anger is in the father's anger." (Tirmidhī)

Kindness to Parents

If our father is upset with us, then Allāh سبحانه وتعالى will be upset with us and if our father is happy with us, then Allāh سبحانه وتعالى will be happy with us.

Abū Hurayrah رضي الله عنه reported that a person came to the Messenger of Allāh صلى الله عليه وسلم and asked: "Who among the people is most deserving of fine treatment from me?" He صلى الله عليه وسلم replied: "Your mother." He then asked, "Who next?" The Prophet صلى الله عليه وسلم replied: "Your mother." He asked again: "Who next?" He صلى الله عليه وسلم said again, "Your mother." He again asked, "Then who?" He صلى الله عليه وسلم said: "Your father." (Ṣaḥīḥ Muslim)

Kindness to Parents

We can see from all these sayings how important it is to obey our parents. If they are upset with us then we will not be able to achieve success. We must try our best to keep them happy. We should pray for them with the du'ā' Allāh سبحانه وتعالى taught us to make for our parents:

رَبِّ ارْحَمْهُمَا كَمَا رَبَّيَانِي صَغِيرًا

O Allāh have mercy on them both as they cared for me when I was small
(Qur'ān 17:24)

Akhlāq

Kindness to Parents

One day three people were on a journey when a storm forced them to take shelter in a cave. A rock slipped down from the mountain and blocked the exit from the cave. Each of them prayed to Allāh سبحانه وتعالى through one of their good actions.

One of them said, 'O Allāh! I had parents who were old, and nobody from the family would be permitted to have any milk until my parents had taken some.

One day, I was delayed in coming to them. I milked the sheep and took the milk to them, but I found them sleeping. I disliked to provide my family with the milk before them, so I waited with the bowl in my hand until the day dawned. Then they got up and drank the milk.

O Allāh! If I did that for Your sake only, please relieve us from the situation we are in through this rock.' The rock shifted a little. (Ṣaḥīḥ al-Bukhārī)

Here's an extract from a poem about mothers:

When you were a one year old, she fed you and bathed you -
You thanked her by crying all night...

When you were two years old, she taught you to walk -
You thanked her by running away when she called...

When you were three years old, she made all your meals with love -
You thanked her by tossing your plate on the floor...

When you were four years old, she gave you some crayons -
You thanked her by colouring on the dining room cloth...

When you were five years old, she dressed you for the holidays -
You thanked her by plopping into the nearest pile of mud...

When you were six years old, she walked you to school -
You thanked her by screaming, "I'M NOT GOING!"

When you were seven years old, she bought you a ball -
You thanked her by throwing it through the
next door neighbour's window...

When you were eight years old, she handed you an ice cream -
You thanked her by dripping it all over your lap...

When you were nine years old, she paid for lessons -
You thanked her by never even bothering to pay attention...

When you were 10 years old, she took you place to place -
You thanked her by running away and never looking back...

When you were 11 years old, she took you shopping -
You thanked her by demanding she buy everything you touched.

Kindness to Parents

Dear children, there's no substitute for our parents. We should cherish every single moment with them. Though at times they may not be the best of friends to us, or agree with our thoughts, they are still our parents who brought us up. We should try to do those things which will make them happy, and in turn we can earn their prayers.

Once gone, only fond memories of the past and regrets will be left.

Speaking the Truth

"O you who believe, fear Allāh, and be in the company of the truthful." (Qur'ān 9:119)

Our Beloved Messenger Muḥammad صلى الله عليه وسلم said: "Keep hold of the truth. Indeed, truthfulness leads to good and good leads to Jannah. A person continues to be truthful until he is registered as truthful in the sight of Allāh سبحانه وتعالى. Stay away from lying, for lying leads to evil, and evil leads to Jahannam. A person continues to lie until he is registered as a liar in the sight of Allāh سبحانه وتعالى." (Ṣaḥīḥ al-Bukhārī)

Ibn 'Umar رضي الله عنه reported that our Beloved Messenger Muḥammad صلى الله عليه وسلم said "When a person lies, the angels move a mile away from him because of the bad odour of what he has uttered." (Tirmidhī)

Speaking the truth is very important. When we don't speak the truth, Allāh سبحانه وتعالى is upset with us, the angels leave our side, and people lose trust.

Speaking the truth will make you the beloved of Allāh سبحانه وتعالى, the angels will surround you, and people will trust you.

A liar always gets caught in the end. In order to cover one lie and to make it seem as the truth, we may need many lies.

Speaking the Truth

A pupil is absent from madrasah (school) because he went to a party.

Let's understand this statement through an example:

Teacher: "Why were you absent yesterday?"

Pupil: "I was not well." (first lie)

Teacher: "O what happened?"

Pupil: "I had a stomach ache and a high temperature." (second lie)

Teacher: "Did you not go to see the doctor?"

Pupil: "Yes I did." (third lie)

Teacher: "Who took you and what did the doctor say?"

Pupil: "My mum took me and the doctor said I had a stomach bug." (fourth & fifth lie)

Teacher: "Did he give you any medicine?"

Pupil: "Yes." (sixth lie)

Speaking the Truth

And we can go on and on. Many a time we feel that through lying we will be saved but it is actually the opposite. Our Beloved Messenger Muḥammad صلى الله عليه وسلم has said, "Speaking the truth will save you and lying will destroy you."

One day, long ago, there lived an emperor in the Far East who was growing old, and knew it was time to choose his successor. Instead of choosing one of his assistants or his children, he decided something different. He called young people in the kingdom together one day. He said, "It is time for me to step down and choose the next emperor. I have decided to choose one of you."

The kids were shocked! But the emperor continued, "I am going to give each one of you a seed today, one very special seed. I want you to plant the seed and water it and come back here one year from today with what you have grown from this seed. I will then judge the plants that you bring, and the one I choose will be the next emperor!"

Speaking the Truth

One boy named Ling was there that day and he, like the others, received a seed. He went home and excitedly told his mother the story. She helped him get a pot and soil, and he planted the seed and watered it carefully. Every day he would water it and watch to see if it had grown. After about three weeks some of the other youths began to talk about their seeds and the plants that were beginning to grow.

Ling kept checking his seed but nothing ever grew. Three weeks, four weeks, five weeks went by and still nothing. By now, others were talking about their plants, but Ling didn't have a plant; he felt like a failure. Six months went by but still nothing grew in Ling's pot. He just knew he had killed his seed.

Everyone else had trees and tall plants, but he had nothing. Ling didn't say anything to his friends. He just kept waiting for his seed to grow.

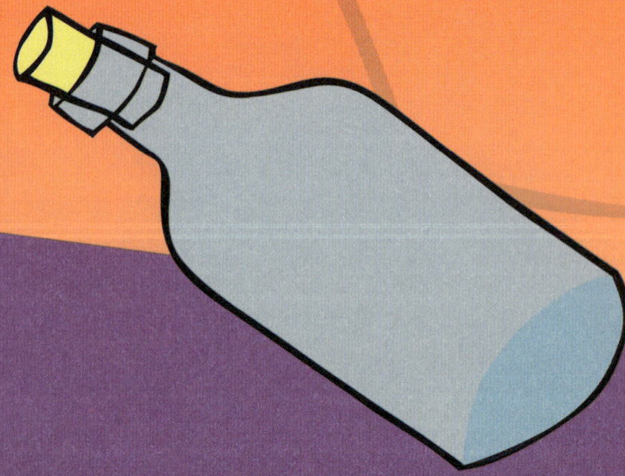

Speaking the Truth

A year finally went by and all the youths of the kingdom brought their plants to the emperor for inspection. Ling told his mother that he wasn't going to take an empty pot. She said, "Be truthful about what's happened my dear son."

Ling knew his mother was right. He took his empty pot to the palace and when he arrived he was amazed at the variety of plants grown by the other youths. They were beautiful and in all shapes and sizes. Ling put his empty pot on the floor and the others laughed at him. A few felt sorry for him and just said, "Hey nice try."

When the emperor arrived, he surveyed the room and greeted the young people. Ling just tried to hide in the shadows. "Wow! what great plants, trees and flowers you have grown," said the emperor. "Today, one of you will be appointed the next emperor!" All of a sudden, the emperor spotted Ling at the back of the room with his empty pot. He ordered his guards to bring him to the front. Ling was terrified and thought, "The emperor knows I'm a failure! Maybe he will have me killed!"

Speaking the Truth

When Ling got to the front, the emperor asked his name. "My name is Ling," he replied. All the kids were laughing and making fun of him. The emperor asked everyone to quieten down. He looked at Ling, and then announced to the crowd, "Behold your new emperor! His name is Ling!" Ling couldn't believe it. Ling couldn't even grow his seed. How could he be the new emperor? Then the emperor said, "One year ago today, I gave everyone here a seed. I told you to take the seed, plant it, water it, and bring it back to me today. But I gave you all boiled seeds which would not grow. All of you, except Ling, have brought me trees, plants and flowers. When you found that the seed would not grow, you substituted another seed for the one I gave you. Ling was the only one with the courage and honesty to bring me a pot with my seed in it. Therefore, he is the one who will be the new emperor!"

Next time someone asks you something, think!
Should I be honest and speak the truth
or should I be dishonest and lie?

Speaking the Truth

Think of the harms of lying.

Allāh سبحانه وتعالى distances a liar from His mercy.

Lying is one of the signs of hypocrisy - where a person is a Muslim on the outside but a disbeliever on the inside.

Lying leads to Jahannam.

People will lose trust in you.

Our Beloved Messenger صلى الله عليه وسلم was so truthful that he was given the title of **'As-Ṣādiq'** (The Most Truthful).

One last point to remember is that lying as a joke is ḥarām too.

It was narrated that Ibn 'Umar رضي الله عنه said, "The Prophet صلى الله عليه وسلم said, "I joke, but I speak nothing but the truth." (Ṭabarāni)

Saying a Good Word

"Not a single word is uttered by one but there is a watcher near him, ready (to record)." (Qur'ān 50:18)

Abū Hurayrah رضي الله عنه reported that our Messenger Muḥammad صلى الله عليه وسلم said: "Whoever believes in Allāh سبحانه وتعالى and the Last Day should speak a good word or remain silent." (Ṣaḥīḥ al-Bukhārī)

The tongue is a blessing from Allāh سبحانه وتعالى. It can bring nations together or it can divide them just as easily.

We must always weigh our words before we utter them.

Words are like arrows: once they leave your mouth the damage is done, but whilst they are still with you, you have control.

The pain felt through words can be more severe than pain felt by other means.

Words are like medicine: a little is enough while too much destroys you.

Saying a Good Word

Our Beloved Messenger Muḥammad صلى الله عليه وسلم **said: "He who remains silent is saved." (Tirmidhī)**

If words were silver, silence would be gold.

Many a time we say things without paying much attention, thereafter we regret those words.

Abū Hurayrah رضي الله عنه **narrates that the Messenger** صلى الله عليه وسلم **said: "A man utters a word pleasing to Allāh** سبحانه وتعالى **without considering it of any significance for which Allāh** سبحانه وتعالى **exalts his rank (in Jannah); another one speaks a word displeasing to Allāh** سبحانه وتعالى **without considering it of any importance, and for this reason he will sink down into Hell." (Ṣaḥīḥ al-Bukhārī)**

Let us ponder over this ḥadīth. A few words said without caution can result in tremendous harm. That is why an intelligent person always thinks before he speaks, whilst a foolish person speaks and then thinks.

We must not blurt out the first thing that comes into our minds. We should consider the consequences and whether we really need to utter these words.

Saying a Good Word

At times some people tease and bully others through their words. Allāh سبحانه وتعالى reminds us in the Qur'ān:

"O you who believe! Let not (one) group laugh at (another) group since maybe they are better than them, nor let women (laugh) at (other) women, since maybe they are better than them; and do not insult one another nor call one another by nicknames. How bad is it, to insult one's brother after having Faith? And whoever does not repent, then it is those who are the wrongdoers." (Qur'ān 49:11)

We do not know how close these people are to Allāh سبحانه وتعالى.We might hurt them with our words and cause harm to ourselves by their broken hearts.

Saying a Good Word

Once a couple sat to dine as the rain pelted against their window panes. Suddenly, a knock came at the door. The wife ran to the door and thought, "Who could it be in such weather?" As she opened the door, she saw a beggar in rags sitting at the doorstep with his hands outstretched saying, "Please for Allāh سبحانه وتعالى's sake give me some food, I am so hungry." The wife felt sorry and went immediately to get some food. But her husband, already angry for being disturbed at his meal time, stood up and marched to the door, looked down at the beggar, gave him one kick and slammed the door in his face...

The beggar made a sigh, looked up to the heavens and moved away.

As years went by, the rich man's business began to deteriorate, and slowly but surely he was close to bankruptcy. He had to tell his wife to leave, for he could no longer afford to keep her. It so happened that he had to sell his house to pay his way through life, but in spite of this, his money soon expired. He was left with nothing except his own clothes and forced onto the streets to beg.

Saying a Good Word

He went from door to door knocking, and asking for some food to keep his back straight, but no one would give him anything. Going on, he arrived at a huge mansion hoping for something from the occupants.

Knock! Knock!

The lady in the house hurried towards the door and as she opened it, she fell down unconscious with a scream. The husband came running to see who had troubled his dear beloved wife and saw a beggar at the door. The husband gave the beggar a lot of food from the house and some money, and he bade him farewell so that he could attend to his wife.

Saying a Good Word

When she regained her senses, she said "Many years ago I sat to dine with my ex-husband and someone similar came to the door. My husband treated him harshly and shooed him away. Now the man that just came to our door was my ex-husband, who once upon a time was rich." The new husband looked at his wife with love and said, "Shall I tell you something more amazing? It was I, the one who knocked on your door those many years ago as a beggar!"

O bullies and oppressors out there take heed for Allāh سبحانه وتعالى says in his Glorious Book:

"Do not think Allāh to be ignorant of the deeds of those who do wrong. He is only giving respite till a day when the eyes shall be fixed in horror." (Qur'ān 14:42)

Turn to Allāh سبحانه وتعالى now before you are forced to be humble.

Saying a Good Word

Another grave sin that occurs through the tongue is ghībah.

One of the main things that causes a person to lose the reward of his actions is the act of ghībah, which is to speak evil about Muslim brothers or sisters behind their backs.

Allāh سبحانه وتعالى has equated backbiting with eating our dead brothers' flesh.

"...do not backbite one another. Does one of you like that he eats the flesh of his dead brother? You would hate it." (Qur'ān 49:12)

On the Day of Judgement, the good deeds of the backbiter will be given to the one whom he spoke ill of.

Saying a Good Word

The Beloved Messenger Muḥammad صلى الله عليه وسلم said to his Companions: "Do you know the one who is bankrupt?" They said, "The bankrupt person is the one who has no money and no possessions." He replied, "Among my Ummah, the one who is bankrupt is the one who will come on the Day of Resurrection with prayer and fasts and zakāh (to his credit), but he will come having insulted this one, slandered that one, consumed the wealth of this one, and shed the blood of that one, and beaten that one. So they will all be given some of his Ḥasanāt (good deeds), and when his Ḥasanāt runs out before judgement is passed, some of their sins will be taken and cast onto him, then he will be cast into the Fire." (Ṣaḥīḥ Muslim)

Imagine how this person will feel. Imagine how we would feel if we spent our whole life saving money only to see it given to other people in front of us. Think! This is what will happen on the Day of Judgement. All the efforts of a person will be wasted away only because he could not control his tongue.

May Allāh سبحانه وتعالى protect us all from this sin and allow us to use good words when we speak.

Ādāb

Learning Objectives

Ādāb

At the end of this unit pupils should be able to:

- List the etiquettes of travelling.
- Recall the etiquettes of studying.
- Mention the virtues of reciting the Qur'ān.
- Describe the sunnah method of walking.
- Demonstrate the ādāb of going to masjid and when inside the masjid.

Ādāb of Travelling

"Then once the ṣalāh (Jumu'ah) is over, disperse in the land, and seek the grace of Allāh, and remember Allāh abundantly, so that you may be successful." (Qur'ān 62:10)

"...Recall the favour of your Lord after having mounted upon it and so you may say, "Pure is the One who has subjugated this for us, and we were not able to have control over it and verily to our Rabb do we return." (Qur'ān 43:13-14)

'Abdullāh ibn 'Umar رضي الله عنه narrates that when Muḥammad صلى الله عليه وسلم used to mount his animal for setting out on a journey, he would say اَللّٰهُ أَكْبَرُ (Allāhu Akbar – Allāh is Great) three times and then pray:

Ādāb of Travelling

سُبْحَانَ الَّذِي سَخَّرَ لَنَا هٰذَا وَمَا كُنَّا لَهُ مُقْرِنِينَ وَإِنَّا إِلَى رَبِّنَا لَمُنْقَلِبُونَ
اللّٰهُمَّ إِنَّا نَسْأَلُكَ فِي سَفَرِنَا هٰذَا الْبِرَّ وَالتَّقْوٰى وَمِنَ الْعَمَلِ مَا تَرْضٰى
اللّٰهُمَّ هَوِّنْ عَلَيْنَا سَفَرَنَا هٰذَا وَاطْوِ عَنَّا بُعْدَهُ
اللّٰهُمَّ أَنْتَ الصَّاحِبُ فِي السَّفَرِ وَالْخَلِيفَةُ فِي الْأَهْلِ
اللّٰهُمَّ إِنِّي أَعُوذُ بِكَ مِنْ وَعْثَاءِ السَّفَرِ وَكَآبَةِ الْمَنْظَرِ وَسُوءِ الْمُنْقَلَبِ فِي
الْمَالِ وَالْأَهْلِ

"Pure is the One who has subjugated this for us, and we were not able to have control over it and verily to our Rabb do we return.
O Allāh we ask You for goodness and taqwā in this journey of ours, and we ask You for deeds which please You. O Allāh, facilitate our journey and let us cover its distance quickly. O Allāh, You are The companion on the journey and the One who looks after the family. O Allāh, I seek refuge with You from the difficulties of this journey, and of witnessing undesirable events and finding undesirable changes in property and family on return."

And when he would return from a journey, he used to say the same words and made this addition:

آيِبُونَ تَائِبُونَ عَابِدُونَ لِرَبِّنَا حَامِدُونَ

"We return repentant to our Lord, worshipping our Lord, and praising our Lord." (Ṣaḥīḥ Muslim)

Ādāb of Travelling

Pray two rak'āt of ṣalāh before departure.

Travel in a group and not alone (unless absolutely necessary).

Appoint one person as the amīr (leader).

Say بِسْمِ اللهِ when boarding a vehicle.

When ascending say: اَللهُ أَكْبَرُ

When descending say: سُبْحَانَ اللهِ

Whilst on a journey, those with extra provisions should think of those who have less and share.

When the purpose for our journey is complete, we should return quickly back to our families.

On returning from the journey, we should try to go to the masjid first, offer two rak'āt ṣalāh, and then go home.

We shouldn't arrive home unexpectedly - instead, we should let people know the time we think we will arrive.

Ādāb of Studying

"Above every possessor of knowledge, there is someone more knowledgeable" (Qur'ān 12:76)

Our Beloved Messenger Muḥammad صلى الله عليه وسلم said, "Whoever treads a path seeking knowledge, Allāh will make easy for him the path to Paradise." (Ibn Mājah)

Our Beloved Messenger Muḥammad صلى الله عليه وسلم said, "The seeking of knowledge is obligatory for every Muslim." (Tirmidhī)

Before you begin learning, make sure to have the correct intentions, for actions are judged according to intentions.

Do not study to become famous or to be treated differently.

Make sure to study only for the pleasure and happiness of our Creator, Allāh سبحانه وتعالى.

Respect the books of knowledge.

Respect the tools of knowledge such as pens and pencils.

Ādāb of Studying

- Respect the teacher.
- Do not raise your voice in the teacher's presence.
- Sit in a respectful manner.
- Listen attentively.
- Revisit the work after the lesson.
- Prepare for the next day by reading what is going to be taught.
- Make du'ā', as knowledge is from Allāh سبحانه وتعالى.
- Do not look down on others who may seem to know less than you.
- Knowledge should make you more humble.
- Spread to others what you have learnt.
- Most important of all, practise what you learn.

Ādāb of Studying

Allāh سبحانه وتعالى gives an example of those who have knowledge and then do not practise upon it in the Qur'ān:

'... like a donkey that carries a load of books...' (Qur'ān 62:5)

The books are of no benefit to the donkey as it is just carrying them. Similarly, if we do not practise what we have learnt then we are just carriers.

رَبِّ زِدْنِيْ عِلْمًا

O Allāh increase me in knowledge. (Qur'ān 20:114)

Ādāb of Qur'ān

"So when you recite the Qur'ān, seek refuge with Allāh against Shayṭān, the accursed." (Qur'ān 16:98)

"Recite what is revealed to you of the Book, and establish ṣalāh." (Qur'ān 29:45)

- Perform wuḍū' before touching the Qur'ān.
- Use a miswāk.
- Sit in a respectful manner.
- Place the Qur'ān respectfully.
- Recite the Qur'ān daily.
- Respect the pages of the Qur'ān.
- Recite in a melodious tone.
- Do not place other books on top of the Qur'ān.
- Do not lean on the Qur'ān.
- Use 'iṭr before recitation.

Ādāb of Qur'ān

Recite Ta'awwudh

أَعُوذُ بِاللهِ مِنَ الشَّيْطَانِ الرَّجِيمِ

I seek refuge in Allāh from Shayṭān, the accursed.

Recite Tasmiyah

بِسْمِ اللهِ الرَّحْمٰنِ الرَّحِيمِ

In the name of Allāh, the Most Gracious, the Most Merciful.

Recite with all the rules of tajwīd.

Keep in mind at all times that these are the words of Allāh سبحانه وتعالى.

Ādāb of Walking

'...do not walk on the earth proudly. Surely, Allāh does not like anyone who is arrogant, proud; and be moderate in your walk...' (Qur'ān 31:18-19)

"Do not walk on the earth in an arrogant style. You can neither tear the earth apart, nor can you match the mountains in height." (Qur'ān 17:37)

Buraydah رضي الله عنه reports that the Messenger Muḥammad صلى الله عليه وسلم said: "Give good news to those who walk to the masājid in the dark, that they will have full light on the Day of Judgement." (Abū Dāwūd)

Walk at the side of the road.

Lower your gaze: do not look at those things which Allāh سبحانه وتعالى has told us not to.

Do not look into any houses, where the doors may have been left open.

Ādāb of Walking

Ensure no harm is caused by your walking.

Spread 'salām.'

Reply to the greeting of another if they greet you first.

Remove harmful things from the road.

If you see someone doing something wrong, tell him nicely.

Invite others to do good.

Do not walk proudly by stamping the feet or walking in a style to show off.

Do not gaze aimlessly and idly whilst walking.

Walk with determination and purpose.

Walk humbly and briskly.

When our Beloved Messenger Muḥammad صلى الله عليه وسلم walked, he lifted his legs with strength, leaning slightly forward and placed his feet softly on the ground. He walked at a quick pace. He did not take small steps. When he walked, it seemed like he was going downhill. (Shamā'il Tirmidhī)

Ādāb of the Masjid

"The masājid belong to Allāh سبحانه وتعالى so do not pray to anyone along with Allāh سبحانه وتعالى."
(Qur'ān 72:18)

Abū Hurayrah رضي الله عنه reports that our Beloved Messenger Muḥammad صلى الله عليه وسلم said that "The most beloved places to Allāh are the masājid..."
(Ṣaḥīḥ Muslim)

Dress appropriately before going to the masjid.

Ensure that you do not enter the masjid just after you have eaten anything which has a strong odour (like raw onions) without cleaning the mouth thoroughly.

Ādāb of the Masjid

Enter the masjid with the right foot.

Recite the du'ā':

اَللّٰهُمَّ افْتَحْ لِيْ أَبْوَابَ رَحْمَتِكَ

O Allāh, open for me doors of Your mercy.

Perform two rak'āt upon entering - this is called Taḥiyyatul Masjid.

Do not talk about worldly matters.

Remain silent in the masjid.

Leave the masjid with the left foot.

And upon leaving recite:

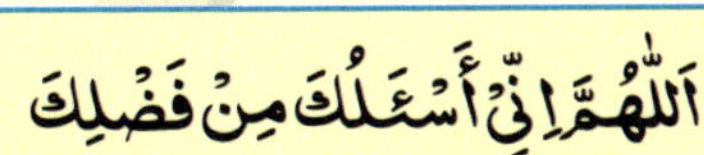

O Allāh, I ask You from Your bounty.

Ādāb of the Masjid

Spend the time in the masjid by:

- Reciting Qur'ān
- Performing ṣalāh
- Remembering Allāh سبحانه وتعالى
- Teaching or learning about our dīn

When you hear the mu'adhdhin calling the adhān, answer the call by repeating the words quietly after him.

When the iqāmah is uttered, rise and walk towards the rows in a calm manner.

Ādāb of the Masjid

If you arrive late and the ṣalāh has already begun, do not run.

We should be considerate of other worshippers by keeping our voices low.

We must avoid talking about worldly matters.

Our Beloved Messenger صلى الله عليه وسلم said "There will come a nation before the end of time, their talk in their masjid will be of worldly matters; Allāh سبحانه وتعالى has nothing to do with such people." (Ibn Ḥibbān)

Bibliography

Fiqh Section

'al-Sughdi (d.461AH), **"al-Nutaf fi 'al-Fatāwā'**, Dar 'al-Furqān, 1984

'al-Samarqandi(d.540AH), **'Tuḥfat 'al-Fuqahā"**, Dār 'al-Kutub 'al-`ilmiyyah, 1994

'al-Kāsānī (d.587AH), **'Badā'i` 'al-ṣanā`i' fī al-Tartīb al-Sharā'ī`'**, Dār 'al-Kutub 'al-ilmiyyah, 1986

'al-Marghinānī (d.593AH), **"al-Hidāyah fī sharh bidāyah 'al-mubtadī'**, Maktabah 'al-Bushra, 2007

'al-Bukhāri, Burhān 'al-Dīn (d.616AH), **"al-Muḥīṭ 'al-Burhānī fi 'al-Fiqh 'al-Nu`mānī'**, Idārah 'al-Qur'ān, 2004

'al-Mawṣilī (d.683AH), **"al-ikhtiyār li ta`līl 'al-Mukhtār'**, 'al-Halabī, 1937

Khusrū (d.885AH), **'Durar 'al-Ḥukkām Sharh Gurar 'al-Aḥkām'**, Dar 'ihyā' 'al-Kutub

Ibn Nujaym (970AH), **"al-Baḥr 'al-Rā`iq Sharh Kanz 'al-Daqā`iq'**, Dār 'al-Kitāb 'al-Islāmī

A-Qudūrī (d.428 AH), **'Mukhtasar 'al-Qudūrī'**, Dār Qubā', 2003

'al-Ṭaḥṭāwī (d.1321 AH), **'Ḥāshiyah 'al-Ṭaḥṭāwī `alā Marāqī 'al-Falāḥ'**, Dār 'al-Kutub 'al-`ilmiyyah, 1997

Ibn `Ābidīn (d.1252 AH), **'Radd 'al-Muḥtār'**, H.M.Saeed

Ḥaydar, Alī (d.1353 AH), **'Durar 'al-Ḥukkām Fī Sharh Majallah 'al-Aḥkām'**, Dār 'al-Jiyal, 1991

Niẓām 'al-Dīn et al, **"al-Fatāwā 'al-Hindiyyah'**, Maktabah 'al-Rashīdiyyah

Ludhyānwi, Mufti Rashīd Ahmed (d.2002 CE), **'Aḥsan 'al-Fatāwā'**, H.M Saeed, 1979

Gangohi, Mufti Maḥmūd 'al-Ḥasan (d.1996 CE), **'Fatāwā 'al-Mahmudiyyah'**, Idārah 'al-Farūq, 2008

Mufti Radhā' 'al-Haq et al, **'Fatāwā Dār 'al-Ulūm 'al-Zakariyyā'**, Zamzam Publishers, 2007

'al-Tatwī, Muhammad Hāshim (d.1174 AH), **'Fākihat 'al-Bustān'**, Dār 'al-Kutub 'al-`ilmiyyah, 2012

Bibliography

Aqīdah Section

'al-Taftāzānī, Sa`d 'al-Dīn (791 AH), '**Sharh 'al-Aqā'id 'al-Nasafiyyah'**, Dār 'al-Bayrūtī, 2007

'al-Ghaznawī (d.773 AH), **'Sharh 'al-Aqīdah 'al-Ṭaḥāwiyyah'**, Dār 'al-Kuraz, 2009

'al-Māturīdī (d.333 AH), **'Kitāb 'al-Tawhīd'**, Dār ṣādir,

'al-Maydānī (d.1298 AH), **'Sharh 'al-Aqīdah 'al-Ṭaḥāwiyyah'**, Dār 'al-Fikr, 1995

'al-Bayjūrī (d.1276 AH) , **'Tuḥfat 'al-Murīd `alā Jawharah 'al-Tawhīd'**, Dār 'al-Salām, 2002

'al-Qārī, Mulla `Alī (d.1014 AH), **'Minaḥ 'al-Rawdh 'al-Azhar Fī Sharh 'al-Fiqh 'al-Akbar'**, Dār a;-Bashā'ir 'al-islāmiyyah, 1998

'al-Qārī, Mulla `Alī (d.1014 AH**), 'Dhaw' 'al-Ma`ālī `alā Manẓūmah Bad'a 'al-amālī'**, Dār 'al-Bayrūtī, 2006

'al-Bạyhaqī (d.458 AH), **'Kitāb 'al-Asmā' wa 'al-ṣifāt'**, 'al-Maktabah 'al-Azhariyyah li 'al-Turāth

'al-Shahrastānī (d.548 AH), **"al-Milal wa 'al-Niḥal'**, Dār 'al-Kutub 'al-`ilmi-yyah, 1992

'al-`Āṣrī, Saif ibn `Alī, **"al-Qawl 'al-Tamām bi Ithbāt 'al-Tafwīdh Mad-haban li 'al-Salaf 'al-Kirām'**, Dār 'al-Fath, 2010

Kan`ān, Muḥammad Aḥmad, **'Jāmi` 'al-La`ālī Sharh Bad'a 'al-'Amāli**', Dār al-Bashā'ir al-Islāmiyyah', 2010

'Al-Nawawī (d.676 AH), **' 'al-Mināj Sharh ṣaḥīḥ Muslim ibn al-Hajjāj'**, Dār 'Ihyā' al-Turāth

Hadīth Section

'al-Bukhārī, Muḥammad ibn Ismā'īl (d.256AH), **'ṣaḥīḥ al-Bukhārī'**, Dar Ṭūq al-Najāh, 2001

Muslim, Muslim ibn al-Hajjāj (d.261AH), **'ṣaḥīḥ Muslim'**, Dār 'iḥyā al-Turāth al-'Arabī,

Nasa'ī, Aḥmad ibn Shu'ayb (d.303AH), **'Sunan al-Nasa'ī'**, al-Risālah, 2001

Abū Dāwūd, Sulaymān ibn al-'Ash'ath (d.275AH), **'Sunan Abī Dāwūd**, Dār al-Risālah al-'ālamiyyah, 2009

Bibliography

'al-Tirmiẓī, Muḥammad ibn `īsā (d.279AH), **'Sunan al-Tirmiẓī'**, Dār al-Gharb al-'islāmī, 1996

'Ibn Mājah, Muḥammad ibn Yazīd (d.273AH), **'Sunan Ibn Mājah'**, Dār al-Risālah al-'ālamiyyah, 2009

Ibn Ḥanbal, Aḥmad (d.241AH), **'Musnad Aḥmad**, Mu'assah al-Risālah, 2001

Al-Ṭabarānī, Sulaymān ibn Aḥmad (360AH), **'al-Mu`jam al-Kabīr'**, Maktabah ibn Taymiyyah,

Al-Ṭabarānī, Sulaymān ibn Aḥmad (360AH), **'al-Mu`jam al-Awṣaṭ'**, Dār al-Ḥaramayn

'al-Bazzār, Aḥmad ibn 'Amr (d.292 AH), **Musnad al-Bazzār'**, Maktabah al-`Ulūm wa al-Ḥikam, 2009

Ibn Ḥibbān, Muḥammad ibn Ḥibbān (d.354 AH), **'Ṣaḥīḥ Ibn Ḥibbān'**, Mu'assah al-Risālah, 1988

Al-Ḥākim, Muḥammad ibn Abdullah (d.405 AH), **'al-Mustadrak alā al-Ṣaḥīḥayn'**, Dār al-Kutub al-`ilmiyyah, 1990

Al-Bayhaqī, Aḥmad ibn al-Ḥusain (d.458 AH), **'al-Sunan al-Kubrā'**, Dār al-Kutub al-`ilmiyyah, 2003

Tārīkh Section

Ibn Kathīr (d.774 AH), ' **'al-Bidāyah wa al-Nihāyah'**, Dār 'Ihyā al-Turath', 1988

Al-Dhahabī (d.748 AH), **'Siyar al-'A`lām al-Nubalā''**, Mu'assah al-Risālah, 1985

'al-Sarjānī et al, **'al-Mawsū`ah al-Muyassarah fī al-Tārīkh al-'islāmī'**, Mu'as-sasah Iqra', 2014

Alkhateeb, Firas, **'Lost Islamic History'**, Hurst Publishers, 2014

'Al-Hassani, Salim et al, **'1001 inventions: Muslim Heritage in Our World'**, Foundation for Science Technology and Civilisation, 2006

Credits

Mawlānā Muḥammad Yaḥyā ibn Fārūq
Director

Mawlānā Muḥammad Qāsim Manjra
Project Manager

Mawlānā Harūn Makda, Mawlānā Isḥāq Boodi and Mawlānā Ẓahīr Sidat
Consultation Panel

'Irfān Chhatbar
Design & Artwork

Shakīl Zikr
Illustration

'Ābid Russell, Rachel Larson & Khadījah Vania
Editing

Bakh Sumira Sulṭān
Workbooks & Extension Activities

Media Jamshidi
Vectorisation

Rest of the team at An Nasihah Publications

May Allāh سبحانه وتعالى reward them all abundantly in this world with blessings and grant them all Jannat al-Firdaws with His everlasting pleasure in the next.

Āmīn.